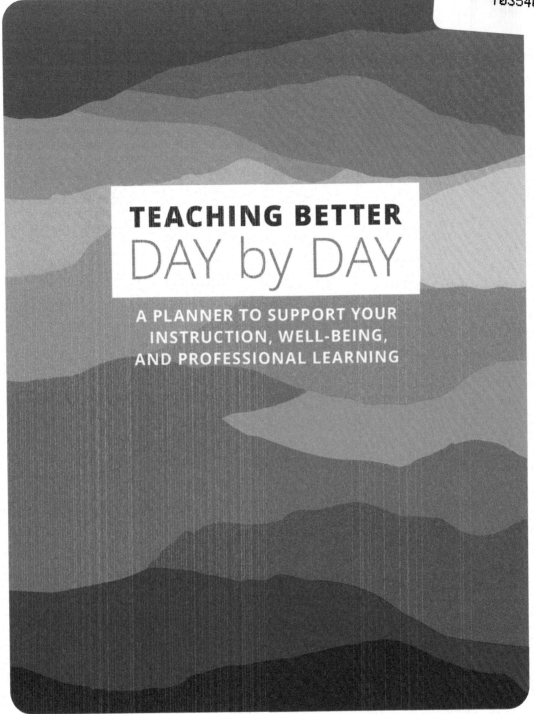

TEACHING BETTER
DAY by DAY

A PLANNER TO SUPPORT YOUR INSTRUCTION, WELL-BEING, AND PROFESSIONAL LEARNING

JIM BURKE

For information:

Corwin
A SAGE Company
2455 Teller Road
Thousand Oaks, California 91320
(800) 233–9936
www.corwin.com

SAGE Publications Ltd.
1 Oliver's Yard
55 City Road
London EC1Y 1SP
United Kingdom

SAGE Publications India Pvt. Ltd.
B 1/I 1 Mohan Cooperative Industrial Area
Mathura Road, New Delhi 110 044
India

SAGE Publications Asia-Pacific Pte. Ltd.
18 Cross Street #10–10/11/12
China Square Central
Singapore 048423

President: Mike Soules
Vice President and Editorial Director:
  Monica Eckman
Executive Editor: Tori Mello Bachman
Content Development Editor: Sharon Wu
Editorial Assistant: Nancy Chung
Project Editor: Amy Schroller
Copy Editor: River Horse Communications
Typesetter: Integra
Proofreader: Dennis Webb
Cover Designer: Gail Buschman
Marketing Manager: Margaret O'Connor

ISBN 9781071910436

This book is printed on acid-free paper.

23 24 25 26 27 10 9 8 7 6 5 4 3 2 1

Contents

Publisher's Acknowledgments

Corwin gratefully acknowledges the contributions of the following reviewers:

Dave Stuart Jr.
Author and Teacher
Cedar Springs, MI

Serena Pariser
Author and Consultant
Minneapolis, MN

Tinisha Shaw
Educator and Academic Coach
Greensboro, NC

 For additional resources related to *Teaching Better Day by Day*, visit the companion website at **resources.corwin.com/daybyday**.

About the Author

 **Jim Burke** is the author of more than 25 books about teaching, learning, and secondary literacy. He taught high school English for more than thirty years, most recently at Middle College High School, a public program located on a community college campus where they emphasized social and emotional learning. He served in leadership positions at the department, school, district, community, state, and national levels, working as an advisor to the College Board AP programs as well as the National Board for Professional Teaching Standards, among others. He is the editor of *Uncharted Territory: A Reader and Guide* (W. W. Norton), author of the *Common Core Companion* books, and co-author with Barry Gilmore of *Academic Moves for College and Career Readiness, Grades 6-12: 15 Must-Have Skills Every Student Needs to Achieve* (Corwin). Jim has received several awards, including the Distinguished Service Award from the California Association of Teachers of English, the National Council of Teachers of English Exemplary English Leadership Award, and the National Intellectual Freedom Award for his work on censorship. In addition, he has worked with Parker Palmer and the Center for Teacher Formation, as well as contributed to several books inspired by Palmer's *Courage to Teach: Exploring the Inner Landscape of a Teacher's Life*. In conjunction with his *Teacher's Daybook* (Heinemann), Jim conducted workshops around the country that focused on personal and professional effectiveness and wellbeing. His most recent efforts have concentrated on social-emotional learning and how those ideas and strategies can help students and teachers flourish in their work.

Introduction: The Energy to Teach

We teach who we are.

—Parker Palmer, *The Courage to Teach: Exploring the Inner Landscape of a Teacher's Life*

Choosing to be curious is choosing to be vulnerable because it requires us to surrender to uncertainty. We have to ask questions, admit to not knowing, risk being told that we shouldn't be asking, and, sometimes, make discoveries that lead to discomfort.

—Brené Brown, *Atlas of the Heart: Mapping Meaningful Connection and the Language of Human Experience*

As the quotation above from Brené Brown reminds us, the work of teachers in recent years has caused us to grapple with a lot of emotions related to vulnerability. I have certainly experienced more than my share of these emotions lately. During the five years it took me to create this planner, I left the traditional public high school where I had taught in-person for more than twenty-five years to take a position in a small public-school program in our district on a college campus where, after only six months, I had to learn to teach all my classes online for more than a year during the COVID-19 pandemic. When we returned a year later, our program was temporarily relocated to a cluster of sad portables in a remote parking lot of the adult school. We now had to teach hybrid classes and we struggled to create lessons that worked with half the class in-person and the other half on Zoom, most of their cameras switched off.

At my new school, I taught only seventy students but shared the responsibility with my other colleagues for managing the school, meeting weekly with the thirty-five advisees we had, and attending the almost daily team meetings we scheduled to discuss everything from the needs of specific students to overhauling the interview process during which we would be meeting with the 160 applicants for the next year. Oh, and of course, we had to create a new curriculum during this period, which entailed a lot of meetings, collaboration, and thinking about what to do, how, why, and by when to do it.

Throughout it all, I was creating this planner, refining it to meet the evolving needs and very real challenges of teaching students who, like your own no doubt, struggled with their mental health in general and in response to the pandemic in particular. By the end of the most recent year, my planner felt like one of those suitcases with stickers all over it, each one not so much a place I had traveled to but a challenge I had faced—and overcome. By year's end, the planner resembled a weathered and heavily stamped passport or much-used journal that documented my adventures, complete with notes from students and photos from memorable occasions (such as my daughter's wedding!) taped here and there to remind me that I cannot teach well if I am not living well outside of school. Each year's *Teaching Better Day by Day* planner is, in other words, both the story of and souvenir that reflects and honors all that I did and learned.

The planner evolved as my own personal and professional needs did during the five years I spent creating it. Some years, in addition to teaching, I served on committees at school or the district level; the past three years I took on responsibility for advising the yearbook, a job that challenged my organizational skills in ways I had not anticipated. During the first year I was creating the early prototype of the planner, I was out for a spell on jury duty during the spring semester. Then, I returned to school only to find out soon thereafter that I had caught a little cancer, which had me out for six weeks and during which I did my best to still plan the curriculum of the course. Through all these challenges and changes, both personal and professional, I found this planner a great comfort and companion. When new situations arose, such as the year I was due for a full, year-long evaluation by our administrators, I turned to this planner to help me manage the different demands. When it did not have the features or functions I needed at such a time, I revised it to better meet not just *my* but *our* needs, for we are in this work together, my friends. Afterall, whatever I need a planner to do, you will no doubt need as well. So, as I designed it, I constantly analyzed my own needs and observed those of my colleagues to better understand and create a planner that would help you better address your needs.

There are few problems that society does not lay at teachers' feet and expect us to solve. A 2021 RAND survey found that teaching has now become *the* most stressful occupation, with teachers almost three times more likely than other adults to report symptoms of depression (Steiner and Woo). Throughout the *Planner* you will find weekly checks and a range of suggested ways to help you protect the energy you need to continue to be the teacher you are.

So, what is this planner offering you? In its pages you will find:

- The **Preparing to Teach** section, which features tools to help you organize essential information (The Teacher's Homepage); track the time, money, and energy that school demands; understand and implement the Six Commitments that form the core of the *Planner* and your work as a teacher; establish both a personal and professional focus for the year ahead; and plan your typical week before the year begins—because to be well, teach well, and work well with others requires that you *be* well yourself.

- **The Year Section**, where you will find the "Look SMARTE" 12-month calendar to help you sketch out or keep track of the year; the "Look Ahead" 12-month calendar where you can make notes for *next* year as you learn your way through the year at-hand; the "Look at the Big Picture" calendar, which encourages you to dream out the next five years of not your classes but your life; and the "Look Long" calendar pages where you will sketch out your units for the current year on your own or in collaboration with your colleagues.

- **The Months Section**, which includes a full two-page monthly calendar; "Personal Professional Development" (PPD) pages where you will find the insights and suggestions of key thinkers about pressing issues, such as Culturally Responsive Teaching, Blended Learning, Disciplinary Literacy, or Social Emotional Learning, along with space to reflect on and apply such ideas to your own classroom; "Work Well" pages designed to facilitate your preparation for the month ahead both personally and professionally by helping you take note of what is working well and what you need to work on; and, finally, a section dedicated specifically to managing your kids, classroom, and curriculum with a different emphasis and set of strategies you can employ each month. In addition to these general features in the Months Section, you will find several pages dedicated to reflecting on the semester just ending and the one to come; these pages appear near the end of the semester and, again, at the end of the year.

- **The Week Section**, where you can identify students of concern; plan out the week for your different classes; identify your priorities using the quad diagram; and, depending on the week, evaluate your well-being or learn how to use one of the six different tools meant to help you be more organized and effective. At the end of each grading period (six weeks), you will find two full pages where you can make notes about the grading period just finishing or the one to come—or both!

- **The Daily Plan Section**, which introduces you to several templates created to help you design effective, engaging, and cohesive units and the individual daily lessons that are the building blocks of such units. Here you will also find examples of how to use the templates and access the digital versions of them, along with samples from my own classes.

I have long been obsessed by the challenges we face as teachers who strive to be effective in the classroom and still maintain a life outside. As a husband who has been happily married for thirty-five years, a father of three now-grown children, and someone who has helped my wife care for her ninety-five-year-old mother during the fifteen years she has lived with us, I am offering you a tool to help you continue to enjoy, find meaning in, and grow in your role as a classroom teacher while maintaining the energy you need to do all the other things you do—or hope to do. This is only the latest and most ambitious iteration of my efforts to manage time, my classes, and my life that has consumed me since I began teaching so long ago.

The *Planner* also offers teachers—and their teams, departments, or schools—a means of collaborating, a way to have the conversations about instruction and all the related aspects of our work that we gather to help each other solve. For example, a team or department might decide ahead of time to read and do some reflecting in response to one of the Personal Professional Development (PPD) readings, such as Jennifer Abrams's *Having Hard Conversations* (2009) or Glenn Singleton's *Courageous Conversations About Race: A Field Guide for Achieving Equity in Schools* (2015). At the meeting, you and your colleagues would use the PPD reading and your own responses to help you and others engage in a thoughtful conversation about how that reading applies to your own class or your department's needs at that time. In addition, those same questions and features throughout the planner that invite discussion with colleagues also provide you with the opportunity to have such conversations with yourself as you reflect periodically on your work and teaching. Such occasions to reflect—at the end of a week, a month, a grading period, a semester—have been a great salvation for me, giving me the time and space, however briefly, to examine my teaching, my relationships, and my own wellbeing.

In his book *Atomic Habits: An Easy and Proven Way to Build Good Habits and Break Bad Ones* (2018), James Clear argues that all deep, sustainable, and crucial improvement comes in tiny increments. Drawing on his study of world-class cyclists, Clear insists that we cannot become suddenly great at something that is complex; rather, as he shows, it is through the small but consistent efforts to improve our performance by just 1 percent each time we step into the classroom (or get on the bike to train or compete) that we advance toward becoming world-class teachers. After thirty-five years in the classroom, having taught just about every level and type of class there is in-person and online, having learned all that I have along the way from books, workshops, conferences, and colleagues,

I can assure you that the best we can do is get just a little bit better day by day—if we make the right effort. Such improvement is not accidental but is, instead, the consequence of purposeful reflection and intentional practice each day, year in and year out.

Though this planner has places where it asks you to jot down a goal, the truth is that it is really the ritual of the jotting—not the goal you jot down—that makes the difference, for as Clear (2018) reiterates throughout his book, "goals are about the results you want to achieve, [but] systems are about the processes that lead to those goals" (p. 23).

Let me be clear and honest here: I have worked hard these many years to crack the secret code of time and teaching, trying every planner and app, every design and device that came along. The truth is, however, that we can never clear the list, empty the inbox, get all those papers graded and entered. The virtue is in the effort we make toward our own ongoing improvement. Of all the books I read in the course of my research for this planner, the one that stands out as the most honest and reasonable is Oliver Burkeman's *Four Thousand Weeks: Time Management for Mortals* (2021), in which he declares that:

> Productivity is a trap. Becoming more efficient just makes you more rushed, and trying to clear the decks simply makes them fill up again faster. Nobody in the history of humanity has ever achieved "work-life balance," whatever that might be, and you certainly won't get there by copying the "six things successful people do before 7:00 a.m." The day will never arrive when you finally have everything under control—when the flood of emails has been contained; when your to-do lists have stopped getting longer; when you're meeting all your obligations at work and in your home life; when nobody's angry with you for missing a deadline or dropping the ball; and when the fully optimized person you've become can turn, at long last, to the things life is really supposed to be about. (p. 13)

The *Teaching Better Day by Day* planner and all that I have done and learned along the way from books, colleagues, and mentors has taught me the truth and usefulness of this passage from Burkeman's book. After all these years in the classroom, I am still learning, still loving the work, still finding through my relationship with my work, my students, and my wife and family, the sense of meaning and purpose that David Whyte (2009) insists is to be found through the "three marriages" to our Work, our Self, and Other people (p. 10).

It is these three "marriages" that are inevitably on my mind (or in my heart) when I sit down on Sundays to reflect on the previous week or begin drafting the week to come. I realize we have all become digital ninjas, able to open and juggle multiple apps simultaneously while sipping our now-lukewarm latte and writing an email to a parent. Planning on paper, using this planner to think about my role, our work, or what I want kids to learn—this is work that benefits from slowing down, from being disrupted just enough to make us the intentional, deliberate, and creative teachers we are or strive to become. As you can see from the examples of my own lessons that you will find in the Daily section, I use the computer to do all sorts of work for my class; however, when I sit down with my own version of this planner and a colleague or members of my team, I don't want a screen between us the whole time. I want to give them my full attention and feel free to engage in the messy thinking that is natural to that phase of our work as teachers. Then, once the ideas have been refined, I will translate my notes from the pages in the planner into the Daily Agenda or unit design template intended for more public use or consumption.

So, think of this planner as a place to compose your curriculum and also to chart the course of your life in the year(s) to come. The new teacher I once was would have been so grateful for the guidance this planner offers. The department chair I was long ago would have found a way to get one for everyone in the department so we could use it for the more focused conversations that the Personal Professional Development feature throughout the *Planner* invites us to have. I would have given one to every student teacher I ever had, for they never arrived with much of a map of the territory from the university that sent them. When I was an instructional coach, meeting with and observing teachers during their evaluation years, I would have used what little money I had available to buy each teacher a copy to help them track and reflect on their progress during the year.

In these ways, I hope anyone using the *Planner* will be better able to locate and keep alive within themselves the "energy to teach" that Don Graves (2001) wrote about in his book by the same name. As he said of the participants in his long-term study of teachers (of whom I was one), "not all teachers suffer from a lack of energy. Some are able to transcend the most difficult circumstances and foster significant learning in their students. There are also teachers who are part of a building or system with a clear vision for learning. They give energy to each other and continually transform goals to match their vision for children" (p. 3).

I hope this planner and the invitations it extends to you can give you the energy that creating and using it has given me these past five years. Our work these days demands that we be agile as we attempt to transform the many challenges we encounter daily into a story which I hope, as you complete each year's *Teaching Better Day by Day* planner, feels rewarding, meaningful, and as important as you and the work you do every day.

PREPARING TO TEACH

What then is a teacher? As teachers we use the many sources of professional knowledge, skill and experience at our disposal to engage the minds and hearts of children and youth by teaching and inspiring them. And once we mess with minds and hearts, we are prepared to take responsibility for the messes we have made, the dreams we inspired, the minds we have brought to life, the prejudices we have forestalled, and the society to which we have given hope. And yet, there's a deeper sense of what it means to take responsibility for the messes that we are destined, nay obligated, to make. We are obliged as teachers to do everything we can to become smarter about our subjects, our students, and our work, more skilled in the pursuit of our practice, and more ethical, self-aware and empathic as human beings that our society trusts to mess with minds and hearts.

—**Lee Shulman** Preface, *What Teachers Should Know and Be Able to Do*

CREATING YOUR HOMEPAGE

Notes and Other Info		
	School Address	
	Main Phone	
	Department Phone	
	School Fax	
	School Email	
	School URL	
	Substitute System	

Fall Semester Schedule

Spring Semester Schedule

Substitute Information

Substitutes

Dates	Reason	Confirmation #	Dates	Reason	Confirmation #

CREATING YOUR HOMEPAGE

Notes and Other Info	FALL SEMESTER				
	Period	Class	Room	Class Size	Note
	SPRING SEMESTER				
	Period	Class	Room	Class Size	Note
	FREQUENTLY USED INFORMATION				

MONITORING YOUR TIME, MONEY, AND ENERGY

DIRECTIONS Use this worksheet to record the hours you spend on committees, professional development, and other tasks you are expected or required to do. Seek compensation for these hours or use this sheet as a record when being evaluated.

Event • Meeting • Work	Date	Start	Stop	Break	Total	Energy *	Notes and Other Info

* In his *The Energy to Teach* (Heinemann 2001), Don Graves asked teachers in the study to rate whatever they did throughout the day as "GE" (Gave Me Energy) or "TE" (Took My Energy).

NOTES

Let's commit ourselves to a few statements that have deep and important roots in research and are statements that any teacher would want their students to be able to say were true of their teacher. These Six Commitments are an essential part of the design of the whole *Teaching Better Day by Day* planner. To flip that, the planner is your guide to *living* these commitments, to honoring and maintaining those commitments to our students, our colleagues, and ourselves. Use the space to the right to evaluate and reflect on where you are when it comes to understanding, making, and sustaining these commitments in the year ahead.

1. **I am committed to the success and well-being of all my students and to their learning.**

   - I believe that all my students can learn and meet my high expectations.

   - I know my students' interests, needs, strengths, and situation in and outside school.

   - I consider the social, emotional, academic, and cultural factors when teaching and assessing students.

   - I provide a range of ways and opportunities for students to learn and demonstrate that learning.

   - I make a dedicated effort to respect, support, and challenge all my students.

2. **I know my subject and how to teach it so that all my students will learn, remember, and enjoy it.**

   - I make an effort to keep my disciplinary and pedagogical knowledge current and comprehensive.

   - I expect students to learn, engage with, and think critically about the core ideas and issues.

   - I know and teach students how my subject is created, organized, and linked to other disciplines.

   - I teach students the disciplinary knowledge and literacies essential to my subject.

   - I use digital tools as authentic ways for students to learn and apply subject matter knowledge.

3. **I am responsible for designing, teaching, and assessing the lessons and learning of all my students.**

   - I consider students' needs when planning for instruction and interpreting assessments.

   - I design my units and lessons as learning progressions with specific intentions.

   - I clarify the specific learning intentions and success criteria—and how these will be assessed.

   - I know and focus on the knowledge and skills I want students to acquire, connect, and transfer.

   - I provide students multiple ways to learn or demonstrate what they have learned.

The Six Commitments constitute the core of the *Teaching Better Day by Day* planner and our work in general. Before the year begins, take some time to reflect on what the Six Commitments really ask of us and what they mean. As you think and write about them, consider which are strengths that can be refined, and which are areas to work on developing this year.

1. I am committed to the success and well-being of all my students and to their learning.

_____
_____
_____
_____
_____
_____
_____
_____
_____
_____

2. I know my subject and how to teach it so that all my students will learn, remember, and enjoy it.

_____
_____
_____
_____
_____
_____
_____
_____
_____
_____

3. I am responsible for designing, teaching, and assessing the lessons and learning of all my students.

_____
_____
_____
_____
_____
_____
_____
_____

4. **I consider equity and access when designing, teaching, and assessing my lessons and students' learning.**

- I evaluate my curriculum and teaching for bias, assumptions, and other possible obstacles to learning.

- I treat students' life experience, languages, knowledge, and culture as assets for learning.

- I ensure that all my students have access to and know how to use digital and print resources to learn.

- I factor the importance of relationships, cognitive scaffolding, and critical social awareness into my instruction.

- I differentiate instruction and assessment as needed to help all students learn and succeed.

5. **I reflect on, analyze, and refine my teaching based on feedback from multiple sources.**

- I revise my instructional goals, plans, and assessments based on data and observations.

- I design my instruction based on established theories and reasoned judgment born of experience.

- I seek and accept feedback based on data and observations from colleagues, administrators, and students.

- I stay abreast of current research and incorporate new findings into my practice when appropriate.

- I value the ability to reason well, examine multiple perspectives, question "the truth," solve problems, and persevere.

6. **I participate in and contribute to my learning community at school and the profession at large.**

- I collaborate with my colleagues and students' families to improve our school and students' learning experience.

- I communicate with colleagues and parents as needed using the appropriate technology tools.

- I engage in ongoing professional development through conferences, workshops, and reading.

- I join, contribute to, and sometimes lead teams, committees, or professional development efforts.

- I share what I learn about teaching, learning, and students with colleagues and families.

4. I consider equity and access when designing, teaching, and assessing my lessons and students' learning.

5. I reflect on, analyze, and refine my teaching based on feedback from multiple sources.

6. I participate in and contribute to my learning community at school and the profession at large.

FINDING YOUR FOCUS: ESTABLISH A PERSONAL VISION FOR THE YEAR AHEAD

As with any journey, we must begin by deciding where we want to go, how we can get there, who can help us get there, and why we want to go there in the first place. Use this page to think about the year to come, taking into consideration both the expected and the unexpected. Use the diagram below to help you find your focus for the year ahead. It is blank, as all the quads throughout the *Teaching Better Day by Day* planner will be, because the story of the year ahead is yours to write, and the themes, motifs, roles, and responsibilities are yours to define. Of course, your life has more than four domains, but this page in this planner asks you to find and focus on the four roles, responsibilities, or relationships in your personal life that will matter to you most in the year ahead.

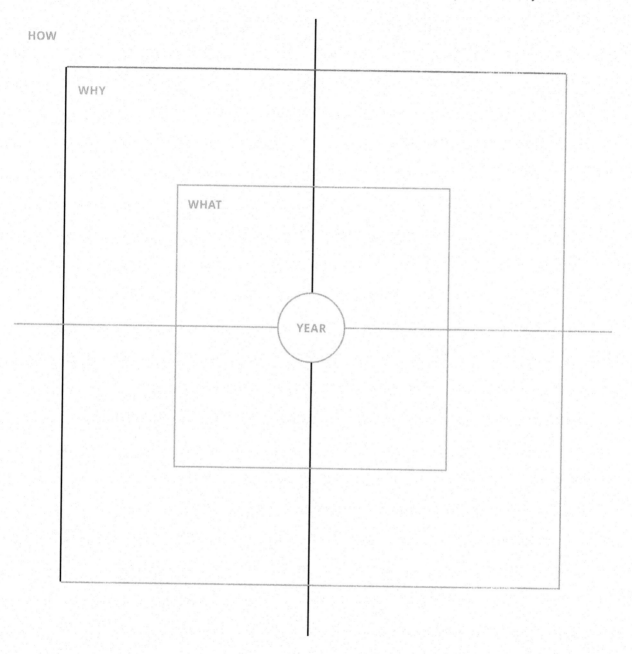

Use the space below to reflect on the contents of your quad above. You might consider starting a separate journal to reflect in greater depth as you move through and compose the story of this year.

_____

_____

_____

_____

_____

Scan the QR code to find a filled-in example of these charts.

FINDING YOUR FOCUS: ESTABLISH A PROFESSIONAL VISION FOR THE YEAR AHEAD

Now is the time to pause and think about where you are in your career and your growth as a teacher. What are the big changes you are preparing for or making this year? How do your essential roles and responsibilities fit in with the other demands of your life and the direction you see yourself taking as an educator in the coming years? Use this page to think about the year ahead, taking into consideration both the expected and the unexpected. Use the diagram, as you did in the PERSONAL version, to help you find your professional focus for the year ahead. It is blank, because the story of the year ahead is yours to write, and the themes, motifs, roles, and responsibilities are yours to define. Of course, your life has more than four domains, but this page in this planner asks you to find and focus on those four roles, responsibilities, or relationships in your personal life that will matter to you most in the year ahead.

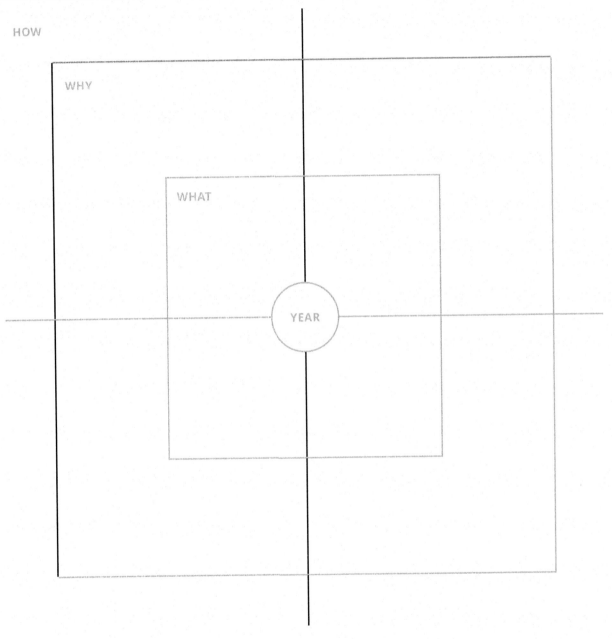

Use the space below to reflect on the contents of your quad above. You might consider starting a separate journal to reflect in greater depth as you move through and compose the story of this year.

Scan the QR code to find a filled-in example of these charts.

TO TEACH WELL *BE* WELL: PLANNING YOUR WEEK

DIRECTIONS: Use this worksheet to help you think more systemically and holistically about your week so you can be sure to have time to plan for and work on those areas of your life you identified as priorities in the FIND YOUR FOCUS pages. Revisit and revise these pages or your time commitments as needed over the course of the year.

Time	Monday	Tuesday	Wednesday
Notes			
5			
6			
7			
8			
9			
10			
11			
12			
1			
2			
3			
4			
5			
6			
7			
8			
9			
10			

Remember: I am committed to doing these three things each week:

Thursday	Friday	Weekend / Notes / To Do

UNDERSTANDING THE SIX CHARACTERISTICS OF AN EFFECTIVE TEAM

Whether you are part of a Professional Learning Community (PLC), an instructional team, or a group created to improve teaching and learning for your department, school, or district, these Six Characteristics offer useful guidelines designed to help you make sure the team you create at the beginning of the year achieves its intended outcomes by the end of that year.

SIX CHARACTERISTICS OF AN EFFECTIVE TEAM	CURRENT RATING			
1. **Structural Conditions:** Does our team have established times that we are able to meet? Are there schedules in place that support collaboration and diminish isolation? Is there availability of needed resources?	4	3	2	1
2. **Supportive Relational Conditions:** Is there trust and respect in place within our team that provides the basis for giving and accepting feedback in order to work toward improvement?	4	3	2	1
3. **Shared Values and Vision:** Do members of the team have the same goal? Do they have shared beliefs about student learning and the ability of team members to impact student learning?	4	3	2	1
4. **Intentional Collective Learning:** Does our team engage in discourse and reflection around sharing practices, knowledge, and skills to impact the growth and achievement of our students? Do we find ways to learn from each other or learn together?	4	3	2	1
5. **Peers Supporting Peers:** Does our team support lifting each other up? Do we celebrate individual and group successes? Do we observe one another while engaged in practice to help others strengthen their practice?	4	3	2	1
6. **Shared and Supportive Leadership:** Are power, authority, and decision making shared and encouraged between teachers and building leaders? Is there a positive relationship among administrators and teachers in the school, where all staff members grow professionally as they work toward the same goal?	4	3	2	1

"The Six Characteristics of an Effective Team," used throughout this planner, was adapted with permission from Fisher, D., Frey, N., Almarode, J., Flores, K., & Nagel, D. (2019). *The PLC+ playbook, grades K–12: A hands-on guide to collectively improving student learning.* Corwin.

UNDERSTANDING THE SIX CHARACTERISTICS OF AN EFFECTIVE TEAM

Use this side of the page to generate ideas for each of the following sections based on your evaluation to the left.

1. Ideas for Maintaining or Strengthening Structural Conditions

2. Ideas for Maintaining or Strengthening Supportive Relational Conditions

3. Ideas for Maintaining or Strengthening Shared Values and Vision

4. Ideas for Maintaining or Strengthening Intentional Collective Learning

5. Ideas for Maintaining or Strengthening Peers Supporting Peers

6. Ideas for Maintaining or Strengthening Shared and Supportive Leadership

THE **YEAR** SECTION

We moved from filling time to spending time. What's the difference? A year of filling time is focused on lessons. A year of spending time is focused on students. We learned to start each year by asking, "How will *these students* be empowered as readers, writers, listeners, and speakers after a year in our care?" This question makes us realize that everything matters: what we plan, how we refine our plans while teaching, how we reflect, and how we decide what comes next. Crafting engaging and relevant learning experiences, combined with the decisions teacher have to make in the moment, defines good teaching.

—**Kelly Gallagher** and **Penny Kittle,** *180 Days: Two Teachers and the Quest to Engage and Empower Adolescents*

LOOK SMARTE: PLAN YOUR YEAR

Use these year-long planning pages to sketch out the broad moves you will make throughout the year. Add key events and holidays that may affect your planning. When you plan, make sure your intended outcomes are **SMARTE**: **S**tudent-centered/**S**pecific, **M**easurable, **A**chievable/**A**ligned/**A**uthentic, **R**ealistic/**R**elevant/**R**esponsive, **T**ransferable/**T**imely, and **E**quitable.

	Month 1		Month 2		Month 3		Month 4		Month 5	
1										
2										
3										
4										
5										
6										
7										
8										
9										
10										
11										
12										
13										
14										
15										
16										
17										
18										
19										
20										
21										
22										
23										
24										
25										
26										
27										
28										
29										
30										
31										

QUICK CHECK: At the end of each month, mark the color that represents your status or how the month went (green = great; red = trouble). In the space below, provide a brief explanation of why you chose the color you did. You might find a concise bulleted list would be enough detail in this case.

PROGRESS NOTES

LOOK SMARTE: PLAN YOUR YEAR

KEEP IN MIND: List the three key areas you are trying to improve on or learn more about this year in your personal and professional life.

	Month 6		Month 7		Month 8		Month 9		Month 10	
1										
2										
3										
4										
5										
6										
7										
8										
9										
10										
11										
12										
13										
14										
15										
16										
17										
18										
19										
20										
21										
22										
23										
24										
25										
26										
27										
28										
29										
30										
31										

QUICK CHECK: At the end of each month, mark the color that represents your status or how the month went (green = great; red = trouble). In the space below, provide a brief explanation of why you chose the color you did. You might find a concise bulleted list would be enough detail in this case.

PROGRESS NOTES

LOOK AHEAD: NOTES FOR NEXT YEAR

Use these year-long planner pages as you move through *this* year to make notes and sketch out plans for what you want to do or change *next* year. Often, we realize as we are teaching a unit in, for example, November, that the holidays undermine our best efforts or that this assignment or unit would be better if done in, say, October.

	Month	Month	Month	Month	Month
1					
2					
3					
4					
5					
6					
7					
8					
9					
10					
11					
12					
13					
14					
15					
16					
17					
18					
19					
20					
21					
22					
23					
24					
25					
26					
27					
28					
29					
30					
31					

REMEMBER: Use the space below to make brief notes about specific reminders or ideas you want to revisit next year. For example, you might make a note about a new unit or text you want to teach, or you may want to jot down a reminder about the ways in which a particular month consistently poses challenges to you or your students' wellbeing as a way of suggesting you try something new next year to disrupt those problems and keep your energy intact.

PROGRESS NOTES

LOOK AHEAD: NOTES FOR NEXT YEAR

KEEP IN MIND: Jot down the three key reminders or changes to revisit next year based on your teaching this year.

	Month		Month		Month		Month		Month	
1										
2										
3										
4										
5										
6										
7										
8										
9										
10										
11										
12										
13										
14										
15										
16										
17										
18										
19										
20										
21										
22										
23										
24										
25										
26										
27										
28										
29										
30										
31										
NOTES										

LOOK AT THE BIG PICTURE: THE NEXT FIVE YEARS

Use these pages to sketch out your personal and/or professional plans for the next few years. Each stage of our life demands different types of planning: taking on new professional roles, starting a family, retiring, pursuing advanced degrees, seeking new positions, or caring for family members. What do you want the coming years to be like? What do you want from them?

Year 1	Year 2	Year 3

LOOK AT THE BIG PICTURE: THE NEXT FIVE YEARS

Year 4	Year 5	Notes

LOOK LONG: UNIT PLANNING FOR THIS YEAR

Use these pages to sketch out units in the early phase of planning. Use the questions in the top left box to guide your thinking. In the spaces below those questions in the first column, you can write the instructional area (e.g., writing), and then in the corresponding area for Unit 1, you could write down the specific standards or other details related to that instructional area. For examples and other ideas, visit the *Teaching Better Day by Day* planner website.

Specific Area(s) of Learning Focus	Unit 1	Unit 2
☐ Identify and analyze the relevant standards. ☐ Determine what knowledge and skills should transfer. ☐ Design the learning progression for this unit. ☐ Develop daily learning intentions for unit lessons. ☐ Define the success criteria for specific standards. ☐ Evaluate this unit or lesson for equity and engagement.		

LOOK LONG: UNIT PLANNING FOR THIS YEAR

Unit 3	Unit 4	Unit 5

YEARLY

LOOK LONG: UNIT PLANNING FOR THIS YEAR

Use these pages to sketch out units in the early phase of planning. Use the questions in the top left box to guide your thinking. In the spaces below those questions in the first column, you can write the instructional area (e.g., writing), and then in the corresponding area for Unit 1, you could write down the specific standards or other details related to that instructional area. For examples and other ideas, visit the *Teaching Better Day by Day* planner website.

Unit 6	Unit 7	Unit 8

LOOK LONG: UNIT PLANNING FOR THIS YEAR

Unit 9	Unit 10	Unit 11

THE **MONTHS** SECTION

That old September feeling, left over from school days, of summer passing, vacation nearly done, obligations gathering, books and football in the air . . . Another fall, another turned page: there was something of jubilee in that annual autumnal beginning, as if last year's mistakes had been wiped clean by summer.

—**Wallace Stegner**, *Angle of Repose*

Academic Moves for College and Career Readiness (2016)
Jim Burke and Barry Gilmore

> "Every discipline comes with its own set of
> what many call 'thinking moves'" (p. 8).

Burke and Gilmore conducted what they call here a "cognitive audit" of their own assignments and the activities, assignments, and assessments found in the Common Core standards, as well as the Advanced Placement, SAT, and ACT documents. They offer detailed explanations of these "moves," then show how to teach and incorporate them into classes across the disciplines.

What to Do

The "A-List" of verbs derived from various standards documents across the disciplines offers a useful menu when designing or evaluating assignments or assessments. These are, in short, the moves students are expected to know and make in all their academic classes. Some terms make greater cognitive demands on students than others, so when designing learning progressions be mindful that students are engaging in more complex work over the course of a unit or the year. The authors' "audit" identified fifteen words or, what they call "academic moves," that are most frequently used and assessed; a second list appears in the appendix of the book that lists "alternative moves that are not so easily tested but nonetheless vital to more innovative and ambitious thinking" (xiii). In addition to advocating for the deliberate and precise use of these fifteen A-List words, the authors emphasize a secondary object: "that the words . . . be used to bring consistency and clarity to the language we all use when teaching or designing assignments within and across disciplines" (xiii).

The A-List: Essential Academic Verbs

Analyze break something down methodically into its parts
break down • deconstruct • examine

Argue provide reasons or evidence to support or oppose
claim • persuade • propose

Compare/Contrast identify similarities or differences between items
delineate • differentiate • distinguish

Describe report what one observes or does
illustrate • report • represent

Determine make a decision or arrive at a conclusion after considering all possible options, perspectives, or results
establish • identify • define

Develop improve the quality or substance of
formulate • generate • elaborate

Evaluate establish value, amount, importance, or effectiveness of
assess • figure out • gauge

Explain provide reasons for what happened or one's actions
clarify • demonstrate • discuss

Imagine create a picture in one's mind; speculate or predict
anticipate • incorporate • predict

Integrate make whole by combining the different parts into one
combine • incorporate • synthesize

Interpret draw from a text or data set some meaning or significance
deduce • infer • translate

Organize arrange or put in order
arrange • classify • form

Summarize retell the essential details of what happened
outline • paraphrase • report

Support offer evidence or data to illustrate your point
cite • justify • maintain

Transform change in form, function, or nature to reveal or emphasize
alter • change • convert

What to Remember

The words students encounter in the directions, questions, prompts, assignments, and assessments are actions. These words identify and emphasize the cognitive processes students are expected to know and be able to do. In addition to emphasizing the role the A-List words play in designing and teaching lessons, the authors highlight the importance of being consistent within departments and across the school when using these terms (and other key words) to avoid confusing students through a Tower of Babel effect.

Equity and Access Check

_____ I define and clarify for all students the key words and actions that appear in the directions of assignments or assessments I give them, making sure they know what the words mean and what it looks like to, for example, "analyze."

_____ I stop to consider whether what I am asking students to do, read, view, or think about would be traumatic for anyone identified as a universal screener.

_____ I monitor those students who are likely to struggle with what I am teaching or the way I am teaching and assess them to see if any require additional support or interventions, such as helping them break down a complex activity into smaller steps as a way of scaffolding the lesson to ensure students' success on it.

_____ I check with students for whom English is not their dominant or primary language to make sure they understand the key words we are using to indicate what they must do on an assignment.

NOTES

MONTH 1

YEAR

LOOKING AHEAD: What is the most important outcome to accomplish by the end of the month—and why?

Notes/Events	Focus 1: What and Why?	Focus 2: What and Why?	Focus 3: What and Why?
	What is your focus and why?	What is your focus and why?	What is your focus and why?

	Focus 1: When and What?	Focus 2: When and What?	Focus 3: When and What?
	When do you work on it and what do you do?	When do you work on it and what do you do?	When do you work on it and what do you do?

The Six Commitments

1. I am committed to the success and well-being of all my students and to their learning.
2. I know my subject and how to teach it so that all my students will learn, remember, and enjoy it.
3. I am responsible for designing, teaching, and assessing the lessons and learning of all my students.
4. I consider equity and access when designing, teaching, and assessing my lessons and students' learning.
5. I reflect on, analyze, and refine my teaching based on feedback from multiple sources.
6. I participate in and contribute to my learning community at school and the profession at large.

Reflect on the one commitment you made the greatest progress on or struggled with the most this month.

HABIT TRACKER DIRECTIONS: List specific **actions** in the left column that will help you develop and maintain healthy habits. Indicate your daily results with a code that works for you. At least some of these habits should be directly related to your three key areas in which you are trying to improve or achieve some specific result this year. Go to jamesclear.com/habit-tracker for more information about tracking your habits.

Habits	1	2	3	4	5	6	7	8	9	10	11	12	13	14	15	16	17	18	19	20	21	22	23	24	25	26	27	28	29	30	31

LOOKING BACK: What did I do just a little bit better this month? How did I do just a little bit better day by day this month?

PROFESSIONAL: Review and reflect on your weekly self-evaluations for the past month.	PERSONAL: Review and reflect on your weekly self-evaluations for the past month.	KIDS: Check In/Check On

MANAGING YOUR KIDS, CLASSROOM, AND CURRICULUM

FOCUS: CLASSROOM ENVIRONMENT

*1. Foster a **classroom environment** in which every student feels known, valued, respected, and safe.*

What This Means and Why It Matters

The "classroom environment" now includes in-person and online spaces, both of which come with potential obstacles that can undermine students' comfort and confidence in the classroom. Students feel known, respected, and safe in classrooms that value their culture, experiences, and knowledge. This means the teacher avoids labels and stereotypes; also, the teacher gathers information on each student's home and academic situation, and their personal and academic needs, including any accommodations the teacher should provide. Bottom line: Beware of anything that might cause a student to feel embarrassed (Newkirk, 2017) and, as a result, undermine their learning and safety in the class. This is what Hammond (2014) refers to in her descriptions of a culturally responsive classroom as cultivating an "ethos of caring" that confirms for students that their environment is "physically, socially, and intellectually safe . . . [so they can enter] a state of relaxed alertness and are primed for learning" (p. 144).

Assess yourself by answering T (True), F (False), S (Sometimes)

_____ I know every student's full name and how to pronounce it.

_____ Every student in my class knows that I respect and care about them, and that I am committed to their safety.

_____ I give each student my full attention and listen to whatever they say without judging what they say or how they say it.

_____ I learn what I can about each student's culture, interests, and needs as a learner and person.

_____ I do not call out or "cold call" students who would be embarrassed or have a panic attack.

_____ I show or express my gratitude for students' contributions, efforts, and progress.

_____ I monitor and solicit students' feedback about how known, valued, respected, and safe they feel in my class and online.

WORK ON: ACADEMIC IDENTITY
HOW TO HELP STUDENTS SEE THEMSELVES AS STUDENTS AND LEARNERS

If the young people who come to school do not see themselves as learners, they are not going to act like learners even if that would help them to be successful in school. It is the teacher's job to help them change their sense of themselves so that studying is not a self-contradictory activity. . . . Academic identity is formed from an amalgamation of how we see ourselves and how others see us. . . . How I act in front of Others expresses my sense of who I am. How others then react to me influences the development of my identity. —Magdalene Lampert, *Teaching Problems and the Problems of Teaching*

MONTH 1   YEAR

NOTES	Monday	Tuesday	Wednesday

CHECK IN • CHECK UP • CHECK OUT

Visit Carol Pelletier Radford's website Mentoring in Action (mentoringinaction.com) for practical suggestions and activities, such as mindfulness meditation, to help you maintain your balance this year.

40

Thursday	Friday	Saturday	Sunday

Culturally Responsive Teaching and The Brain: Promoting Authentic Engagement and Rigor Among Culturally and Linguistically Diverse Students (2014)
Zaretta Hammond

> "Culture, it turns out, is the way that every
> brain makes sense of the world" (p. 22).

Hammond seeks to clear up the "confusion over what culturally responsive teaching (CRT) is and how it works" (p. 4) by "expanding teachers' vocabulary for talking about CRT, especially for underperforming culturally and linguistically diverse students" (p. 5). Her primary means of achieving these important outcomes is her Ready for Rigor Framework, which cultivates students' "intellective capacity," which Hammond defines as "the increased power the brain creates to process complex information more effectively" (p. 16). Though Hammond's framework is more detailed, she organizes it into four "practice areas of CRT" that "set the stage for helping students move from being dependent learners to self-directed, independent learners" (p. 16). These four areas are interdependent, for only when they are integrated do they "create the social, emotional, and cognitive conditions that allow students to more actively engage and take ownership of their learning process" (p. 18). Each of the following four practice areas of the framework are connected through the principles of brain-based learning.

Practice Area 1: Awareness. In the Ready for Rigor Framework, awareness means situating one's instruction within the sociopolitical context that recognizes "that we live in a racialized society that gives unearned privilege to some while others experience unearned advantage because of race, gender, class, or language" (p. 18).

Practice Area 2: Learning Partnerships. Fostering these partnerships requires teachers to "[build] trust with students across differences so that the teacher is able to create a social-emotional partnership for deeper learning" (p. 19).

Practice Area 3: Information Processing. Here, the teacher focuses on "the process, strategies, tactics, and tools for engaging students in high-leverage social and instructional activities that over time build higher order thinking skills" (p. 19).

Practice Area 4: Community Building. This practice requires teachers to create an environment that is social and intellectually safe for dependent learners by establishing and maintaining an environment that "communicates care, support, and belonging in ways that students recognize" (p. 20).

What to Do

Well, the first thing to do is buy and read Hammond's book cover to cover! In the meantime, however, here is one concept worth thinking about and using in your class today. In Practice Area 1: Awareness, Hammond identifies several things to be cognizant of, including "the three levels of culture." After considering these three levels of culture, reflect on which level(s) best describe your current level of understanding:

☐ **Surface Culture**: You know observable, concrete elements, such as food, dress, music, and holidays, most of which are not a source of anxiety or other emotions.

- ☐ **Shallow Culture**: You are familiar with the "unspoken rules around everyday social interactions and norms" (p. 22), such as customs, attitudes toward elders, time, space, values, nonverbal communication, touching, or similar gestures, that are the basis of rapport and trust between people. These are often a source of strong emotion.
- ☐ **Deep Culture**: You know of and understand the knowledge and assumptions that govern students' worldview. This includes ethics, spirituality, health, and group dynamics (competitive vs. cooperative). Deep culture is the foundation of students' self-concept, group identity, and approach to problem solving and decision making.

What to Remember

Hammond reiterates the vital role of the classroom and the culture we create within it for students and how those interact with the brain: "In culturally responsive pedagogy, the classroom is a critical container for empowering marginalized students. It serves as a space that reflects the values of trust, partnership, and academic mindset that are at its core" (p. 143).

Equity and Access Check

____ I define and clarify for all students the expectations, processes, strategies, tactics, and tools I will use (or ask them to use), including my rationale for why I am choosing and using them.

____ I provide models and demonstrate for students what learning and success on tasks or assignments looks like, so that they understand that we are partners in their learning process.

____ I monitor the progress and needs of students whose past experiences have often left them feeling marginalized as learners due to their race, gender, class, or language.

____ I provide a range of interventions, including meeting with students individually or in small groups to understand their needs and develop ways to help them access, learn, or demonstrate their mastery of the content.

____ I monitor and adjust as needed my own assumptions, mindset, actions, and language to avoid any "negativity bias" that would undermine students' learning, performance, or sense of belonging in the community we are creating as a class together.

NOTES

WORK WELL: PREPARE FOR THE MONTH AHEAD

MONTH 2

YEAR

LOOKING AHEAD: What is the most important outcome to accomplish by the end of the month—and why?

Notes/Events	Focus 1: What and Why?	Focus 2: What and Why?	Focus 3: What and Why?
	What is your focus and why?	What is your focus and why?	What is your focus and why?

	Focus 1: When and What?	Focus 2: When and What?	Focus 3: When and What?
	When do you work on it and what do you do?	When do you work on it and what do you do?	When do you work on it and what do you do?

The Six Commitments

1. I am committed to the success and well-being of all my students and to their learning.
2. I know my subject and how to teach it so that all my students will learn, remember, and enjoy it.
3. I am responsible for designing, teaching, and assessing the lessons and learning of all my students.
4. I consider equity and access when designing, teaching, and assessing my lessons and students' learning.
5. I reflect on, analyze, and refine my teaching based on feedback from multiple sources.
6. I participate in and contribute to my learning community at school and the profession at large.

Reflect on the one commitment you made the greatest progress on or struggled with the most this month.

HABIT TRACKER DIRECTIONS: List specific **actions** in the left column that will help you develop and maintain healthy habits. Indicate your daily results with a code that works for you. At least some of these habits should be directly related to your three key areas in which you are trying to improve or achieve some specific result this year. Go to jamesclear.com/habit-tracker for more information about tracking your habits.

Habits	1	2	3	4	5	6	7	8	9	10	11	12	13	14	15	16	17	18	19	20	21	22	23	24	25	26	27	28	29	30	31

PROFESSIONAL: Review and reflect on your weekly self-evaluations for the past month.	**PERSONAL:** Review and reflect on your weekly self-evaluations for the past month.	**KIDS:** Check In/Check On

MANAGING YOUR KIDS, CLASSROOM, AND CURRICULUM

FOCUS: TEACHER-STUDENT RELATIONSHIPS

*2. Develop and maintain **a strong, supportive, rich relationship** with each student.*

What This Means and Why It Matters

Hattie (2009) found the teacher-student relationship has a strong impact on classroom management. Such relationships depend on the teacher being an effective listener, showing empathy, showing they care about the student, and having a positive attitude. Hattie (2009) found the following variables had a strong effect on teacher-student relationships: nondirectivity (letting students choose, initiate, and regulate their learning activities); empathy; warmth; encouragement of higher-order thinking; and encouraging learning (p. 119). Hammond (2014) uses the term "learning partnerships" (p. 75) to describe culturally responsive relationships, which she defines as "anchored in affirmation, mutual respect, and validation that breeds an unshakable belief that marginalized students not only *can* but *will* improve their school achievement" (p. 75). Smith, Fisher, and Frey (2015) identify four elements of strong relationships: trust, respect, optimism, and intentionality, this last item meaning that the teacher "consciously implement[s] sound practices that get results (p. 22).

Assess yourself by answering T (True), F (False), S (Sometimes)

____ I make room for student choice and voice whenever possible.

____ Students know that I am in control of the class but that I see them as partners with whom I collaborate to maintain that order.

____ I use the HALT acronym to monitor and assess my students' well-being: Is this student **H**ungry? **A**ngry? **L**onely? **T**ired? I follow up with them or their counselor as needed so that they know I care, and they can trust me.

____ I avoid any language that would undermine their trust in me or suggest that I do not care about or respect them. This includes knowing and honoring how they prefer to be identified (e.g., name, pronouns, gender, culture, race).

____ I show a sincere interest in not only their academic success but also their interests, activities, talents, and ideas about the world outside the classroom by asking about their health, their recent soccer game, or the concert they recently attended or performed in.

____ I offer each student feedback, recognition, praise, and encouragement in ways that best suit their needs and what I know means the most and is most effective with them.

WORK ON: WORK-LIFE BALANCE
THE CHALLENGE OF PERSONAL/PROFESSIONAL BALANCE

We balance our lives between school and home every day. Even if we are not married or have children, we go home to a world that beckons with its choices. Sometimes we are so busy in both worlds that we aren't conscious of any separation. How well I recall a Saturday morning pushing my half-filled cart around the corner of an aisle in the supermarket and meeting Tony, one of my students . . . who said, "Mr. Graves!" He was startled . . . to find I had an existence apart from school. He examined [the contents of my cart] and looked up with an unspoken judgment, "You even eat food!" —Donald Graves, *The Energy to Teach*

	MONTH 2		YEAR
NOTES	**Monday**	**Tuesday**	**Wednesday**

CHECK IN • CHECK UP • CHECK OUT

Visit Brené Brown's website (brenebrown.com) for some research-based insights and humor to help you when you are "white-knuckling" it through the days. Read, watch, listen—or just feed your soul.

Thursday	Friday	Saturday	Sunday

MONTH 2

Having Hard Conversations (2009)
Jennifer Abrams

> "Hard conversations are never not hard. They will, for the most part, be awkward, uncomfortable, and require us to participate in experiences we would rather avoid. Yet the discomfort we might experience doesn't give us license not to have them" (p. 97).

Abrams identifies the root of our discomfort with having difficult conversations: "we don't like to have hard conversations [because] for the most part, teachers just aren't a confrontational group. . . . Relationships are everything in [our] field. We actively shy away from causing bad feelings" (p. 2). Yet, as Abrams emphasizes, such conversations are essential to our personal and professional growth. If we cannot engage in hard conversations, we cannot make the difference we desire in our departments, professional learning communities (PLCs), or school.

Abrams identifies three key principles, which she dubs the Three Cs: the importance of **clarity**, the centrality of **craft**, and the essential role of **communication**. Near the end of the book, Abrams sums up the process as she uses it in her work as a teacher and coach:

(1) Get Clear: Know why you hesitate to have such hard conversations and what the right question is and the best time to ask it.

(2) Craft: Find the professional language and develop a plan that will lead to the desired outcome for everyone involved.

(3) Communicate: Come up with the words, written out in a script if necessary, that will help everyone to have this hard conversation, and be deliberate about what the "whats, wheres, and whens" of a conversation.

What to Do

Every page of Abrams's book offers practical solutions and suggestions she has tried and refined in her own work with teachers and students. One approach, which you can try on the opposite page, is to create an "outcome map." Abrams describes this as a tool that "will help you to navigate the more complex landscape of affecting change" (p. 46). Answer the following questions on the outcome map in the order they are presented; do not skip any questions.

1. What is the presenting problem? (Paraphrase the problem into a clear, concise statement.)

2. What is the tentative outcome? (Articulate the solution concretely. What would you like to see happening instead of what is currently happening [existing state to desired state]? What is your best outcome?)

3. What would the employee's desired behaviors be if the problem were solved? (What specific and measurable things would you like to see or hear when the problem is solved? Keep the statement focused on behaviors one can see, hear, and repeat.)

4. What would the employee need to know and be able to do to implement the desired behaviors (internal resources)? To implement these behaviors, what knowledge, skills, or awareness would this person need?

5. What are some strategies you could use to help the person build up his or her resources and implement the desired behaviors? (What are some of the specific things you could do to address the needs? Given what you know about the person, what language or actions might help them with the desired behaviors?)

6. What are some of the resources you need in order to execute the strategies above (internal resources)? (In order for you to carry out the strategies, what do you need to learn or relearn? What type of personal support do you need? What is your hunch about what emotion or value you need to tap into to be most effective?)

What to Remember

Learning to initiate or participate in necessary hard conversations is the beginning of each teacher taking a more active role in their department, PLC, or school. It is only a beginning, however, because one quickly realizes, as Abrams points out at the end, that they must move away from "the role of speaker in these hard conversations and [toward] the role of the listener" (p. 99). We must all "build our capacity to courageously listen when we are on the receiving end of a hard conversation . . . to sit with the discomfort and not become defensive or paralyzed" (p. 99).

Equity and Access Check

____ I define and clarify for myself and others what I am trying to say or accomplish, why, and how my comments, requests, or actions will serve the needs of my students in this situation.

____ I provide data, evidence, or examples to support what I am saying and how it will help students.

____ I initiate hard conversations with colleagues, specialists, and school administration about which students are struggling, the reasons, and possible solutions to consider.

____ I advocate for a team-based approach to having and working through these hard conversations.

NOTES

WORK WELL: PREPARE FOR THE MONTH AHEAD

MONTH 3

YEAR

LOOKING AHEAD: What is the most important outcome to accomplish by the end of the month—and why?

Notes/Events	Focus 1: What and Why?	Focus 2: What and Why?	Focus 3: What and Why?
	What is your focus and why?	What is your focus and why?	What is your focus and why?

	Focus 1: When and What?	Focus 2: When and What?	Focus 3: When and What?
	When do you work on it and what do you do?	When do you work on it and what do you do?	When do you work on it and what do you do?

The Six Commitments

1. I am committed to the success and well-being of all my students and to their learning.
2. I know my subject and how to teach it so that all my students will learn, remember, and enjoy it.
3. I am responsible for designing, teaching, and assessing the lessons and learning of all my students.
4. I consider equity and access when designing, teaching, and assessing my lessons and students' learning.
5. I reflect on, analyze, and refine my teaching based on feedback from multiple sources.
6. I participate in and contribute to my learning community at school and the profession at large.

Reflect on the one commitment you made the greatest progress on or struggled with the most this month.

HABIT TRACKER DIRECTIONS: List specific **actions** in the left column that will help you develop and maintain healthy habits. Indicate your daily results with a code that works for you. At least some of these habits should be directly related to your three key areas in which you are trying to improve or achieve some specific result this year. Go to jamesclear.com/habit-tracker for more information about tracking your habits.

Habits	1	2	3	4	5	6	7	8	9	10	11	12	13	14	15	16	17	18	19	20	21	22	23	24	25	26	27	28	29	30	31

LOOKING BACK: What did I do just a little bit better this month? How did I do just a little bit better day by day this month?

PROFESSIONAL: Review and reflect on your weekly self-evaluations for the past month.	PERSONAL: Review and reflect on your weekly self-evaluations for the past month.	KIDS: Check In/Check On

MANAGING YOUR KIDS, CLASSROOM, AND CURRICULUM

FOCUS: CLASSROOM RULES, ROUTINES, ROLES, AND RESPONSIBILITIES

3. Establish **classroom rules, routines, roles, and responsibilities** *that are clear, fair, and beneficial to all students.*

What This Means and Why It Matters

No one can learn (or teach) in a classroom that is chaotic, or that lacks the fair and consistent application of clearly stated rules needed to ensure students feel safe, engaged, and able to succeed. Studies suggest students in grades 6–12 can remember about seven rules and procedures that are clear, memorable, and equitable; K–5 teachers should have five to eight rules and procedures that all students can understand, remember, and follow. Such rules, roles, and responsibilities typically apply to the following categories: behavioral expectations in-class and online; routines at the beginning and end of the class day or period; transitions and interruptions; materials and equipment (especially computers); group work (in-class and online); and seatwork and teacher-led activities that may be in-person or online—or a blend of both. Hattie (2009) found that such rules and procedures, when negotiated with students, had a significant effect.

Assess yourself by answering T (True), F (False), S (Sometimes)

_____ I limit my rules and procedures to six to eight so we can all remember what they are and I can apply them consistently.

_____ I explain the reason for each rule or procedure, then invite students to offer feedback, which I take seriously and make sure students see I am listening to.

_____ I apply these rules and procedures (in-class and online) consistently and fairly to all my students; in addition, I post and refer to them regularly to reinforce them for students.

_____ I have clear rules and procedures regarding in-class and online handling of materials, tools, applications, submitting work, late work, and cell phone usage.

_____ I have an established and effective routine in-place for beginning the class, taking roll, and ending the period.

_____ I communicate homework in-class and online in a clear and timely manner via means all students know how to access.

WORK ON: MINDSET
UNDERSTANDING WHO YOUR STUDENTS ARE AND WHAT THEY NEED TO SUCCEED

Believing that your qualities are carved in stone—the *fixed mindset*—creates an urgency to prove yourself over and over. If you have only a certain amount of intelligence, a certain personality, and a certain moral character—well, then you'd better prove that you have a healthy dose of them. . . . The *growth mindset* is based on the belief that your basic qualities are things you can cultivate through your efforts. Although people may differ in every which way—in their initial talents and aptitudes, interests and temperaments— everyone can change and grow through application and experience. —Carol Dweck, *Mindset*

NOTES	Monday	Tuesday	Wednesday

CHECK IN • CHECK UP • CHECK OUT

Visit James Clear's website (jamesclear.com/articles) to learn more about habits and other strategies to improve your well-being and productivity. These incredible resources are available for free.

READ • REFLECT • RESPOND How do Dweck's ideas about mindset apply to your class, curriculum, and students?

Thursday	Friday	Saturday	Sunday

Blended Learning in Grades 4–12: Leveraging the Power of Technology to Create
Student-Centered Classrooms (2012)
Catlin R. Tucker

Blended Learning in Action: A Practical Guide Toward Sustainable Change (2017)
Catlin R. Tucker, Tiffany Wycoff, and Jason T. Green

> "The ultimate goal of a blended learning class should
> be twofold: (1) allow the teacher to continue working
> directly with students and (2) use an online component
> to develop a learning community that works together
> to discover knowledge." (Tucker, 2012, p. 8)

In *Blended Learning in Grades 4–12* (2012), Tucker defines blended learning as an approach to teaching and learning that "weaves various instructional mediums into a cohesive whole . . . [that combines] traditional face-to-face instruction with an online component" (p. 11). Though initiated in response to the "demand on teachers to do more with less" (p. 11), blended instruction has evolved into "a true community of learners who have vested participation in the ultimate manifestation of the learning environment and experience" (Tucker et al., 2017, p. 8). Though it has important implications for school-wide culture, the focus here is on how it applies to the teacher's classroom.

In *Blended Learning in Action*, the authors identify five teaching and learning best practices that are present in an effective blended learning classroom:

- Personalization (providing unique pathways for each student)
- Agency (involving learners in key decisions about their learning experience)
- Authentic Audience (offering opportunities to create for real audiences)
- Connectivity (allowing students to learning by collaborating with peers and experts both locally and globally)
- Creativity (designing opportunities that allow students to make things but also build skills they will need in the future)

Tucker (2012) advocates for a community-of-inquiry framework, described as "a group of individuals who share a common interest or physical space and engage in a question-driven search for truth and knowledge" (p. 22). She identifies three components of this framework that are essential to the success of such a student-centered blended learning classroom that places a priority on student voice and discussion: (1) social presence (students develop social presence online through meaningful relationships with others); (2) teaching presence (teachers combine direct instruction, curriculum design, and role as online facilitator); (3) cognitive presence (students explore, construct, and confirm their understanding in collaboration with others in-class and online, and reflect on the process).

What to Do

Tucker, Wycoff, and Green (2017) identify several models of blended learning to consider using:

- **Rotation Model**: Students rotate on a fixed schedule or at the teacher's discretion from one station, context, or modality to the next, at least one of which is online.

- **Station Rotation Model**: Students move between multiple learning stations in the classroom, at least one of which requires online learning.

- **Whole Group Rotation Model**: Students rotate between offline and online work, learning on devices available to all in the class, everyone engaging in a common activity at the same time.

- **The Flipped Classroom**: Students do more of the learning online at home to improve their comprehension and ability to apply lessons, then practice and apply the learning in the classroom where they can get more immediate feedback and collaborate with others.

- **Individual Playlist Model**: Students move between a "playlist" of digital and offline learning opportunities or environments according to their needs, preferences, and schedules; they do not necessarily rotate to all the options available to them.

What to Remember

Tucker, Wycoff, and Green (2017) remind us that while students know how to use computers, we need to "instruct them on the purposeful use of [technology] in an academic setting" (p. 104). Learning to use and manage online resources and learning platforms challenges students and teachers alike.

Protocols for onboarding teachers and students are essential, as is ongoing support on how best to implement the models and frameworks associated with blended learning.

Equity and Access Check

_____ I define and clarify for all students what I am teaching them to do, why I am teaching it, and how they will learn and demonstrate that learning using specific models or configurations.

_____ I provide models, and demonstrate for students the role they will play, the techniques, strategies, or technology tools they will use—and how to use them in the context of this lesson.

_____ I monitor those students who are likely to struggle with what I am teaching or the way I am teaching and assessing their performance; I intervene as need to help them learn or participate.

_____ I provide a range of interventions––individual, small group, whole class––based on my observations of their work in the different configurations, their understanding of the content, and their ability to use the computer or software applications as directed.

_____ I gather information about students' access to computers, Wi-Fi, and software applications at home before assigning "flipped" assignments that require them to complete work at home.

NOTES

WORK WELL: PREPARE FOR THE MONTH AHEAD

MONTH 4

YEAR

LOOKING AHEAD: What is the most important outcome to accomplish by the end of the month—and why?

Notes/Events	Focus 1: What and Why?	Focus 2: What and Why?	Focus 3: What and Why?
	What is your focus and why?	What is your focus and why?	What is your focus and why?

	Focus 1: When and What?	Focus 2: When and What?	Focus 3: When and What?
	When do you work on it and what do you do?	When do you work on it and what do you do?	When do you work on it and what do you do?

The Six Commitments

1. I am committed to the success and well-being of all my students and to their learning.
2. I know my subject and how to teach it so that all my students will learn, remember, and enjoy it.
3. I am responsible for designing, teaching, and assessing the lessons and learning of all my students.
4. I consider equity and access when designing, teaching, and assessing my lessons and students' learning.
5. I reflect on, analyze, and refine my teaching based on feedback from multiple sources.
6. I participate in and contribute to my learning community at school and the profession at large.

Reflect on the one commitment you made the greatest progress on or struggled with the most this month.

HABIT TRACKER DIRECTIONS: List specific **actions** in the left column that will help you develop and maintain healthy habits. Indicate your daily results with a code that works for you. At least some of these habits should be directly related to your three key areas in which you are trying to improve or achieve some specific result this year. Go to jamesclear.com/habit-tracker for more information about tracking your habits.

Habits	1	2	3	4	5	6	7	8	9	10	11	12	13	14	15	16	17	18	19	20	21	22	23	24	25	26	27	28	29	30	31

MONTH 4

LOOKING BACK: What did I do just a little bit better this month? How did I do just a little bit better day by day this month?

PROFESSIONAL: Review and reflect on your weekly self-evaluations for the past month.	PERSONAL: Review and reflect on your weekly self-evaluations for the past month.	KIDS: Check In/Check On

MANAGING YOUR KIDS, CLASSROOM, AND CURRICULUM

FOCUS: CLASSROOM ENVIRONMENT

*4. Develop a **mindset** in yourself and your students that emphasizes growth, grit, character, and high expectations.*

What This Means and Why It Matters

Effective teachers emphasize individual self-efficacy, which refers to the student's belief that they can do what is required to succeed—or learn what they need to know. Such students are confident in their work, their ability to learn, themselves, and their teachers and their methods. Engaging, effective classrooms emphasize not only individual student efficacy but collective efficacy, which asks us "to believe that we can make an impact on each and every one of our students" (Fisher et al., 2020, 10). Dweck (2007) emphasizes the importance of the "growth mindset," which means a student perseveres with the belief that with the right type and amount of effort they can learn and succeed. Duckworth (2016) calls this mental disposition "grit," which she defines as *passion* and sustained *persistence* applied toward long-term goals, without worrying about rewards or recognition along the way. Hammond (2014) describes such students' dispositions as an "academic mindset" (p. 109) that highlights the extent to which a student (1) feels they can succeed; (2) believes their ability and competence will grow as a result of their effort; (3) finds value in the work; and (4) sees themselves as belonging to the academic community of a specific class or school.

Assess yourself by answering T (True), F (False), S (Sometimes)

_____ I enter the classroom each day believing that *all* of my students can do (or learn to do) what I ask or assign.

_____ I avoid using any labels to describe my students.

_____ I emphasize effort over ability, validate students' progress, and say "Not yet" instead of "Not able."

_____ I promote a growth mindset instead of a fixed mindset through my actions, words, assessments, and assignments.

_____ I refer to obstacles and errors as opportunities to learn.

_____ I establish and reinforce high expectations, which I then use to design assignments and choose the best approaches to help my students meet.

_____ I offer praise that focuses on students' actions not their traits.

_____ I have students assess and monitor their mindset and grit throughout the year and during challenging assignments.

WORK ON: FOCUSING ON THE ESSENTIALS
THE CORE OF YOUR CURRICULUM

[W]hat is truly "essential" for schools? The evidence points hard to three fundamental elements: reasonably coherent curriculum (*what* we teach); soundly structured lessons (*how* we teach); and large amounts of purposeful reading and writing in every discipline (*authentic literacy*—integral to both what and how we teach). —Mike Schmoker, *Focus: Elevating the Essentials to Radically Improve Student Learning*

MONTH 4   YEAR

NOTES	Monday	Tuesday	Wednesday

CHECK IN • CHECK UP • CHECK OUT

Visit the Calm website (www.calm.com/schools) or app to learn more about their free offer to teachers. I have used it for several years and find it a great source of . . . calm.

Thursday	Friday	Saturday	Sunday

MONTH 4

Disciplinary Literacy: Reading, Writing, Thinking, and Doing . . . Content Area by Content Area (2016)
ReLeah Lent

> "Teachers must be free to employ the tools, texts, and principles of their discipline to give students opportunities to use and apply knowledge" (p. 8).

For years, teachers across all content areas have been told that "all teachers are reading teachers" and that "all teachers must teach writing." In her book *Disciplinary Literacy*, Lent argues and illustrates what it looks like to "[recognize] that reading, writing, thinking, reasoning, and doing within each is unique—and leads to the understanding that every field of study creates, communicates, and evaluates knowledge differently" (p. 1).

Disciplinary literacy empowers content-area teachers to choose, use, and model for their students the way scientists, mathematicians, historians, or economists actually read, write, and think. Lent examines how and why a strategy such as making inferences about literature or nonfiction texts in an English classroom differs from the way scientists make sense of data, economists interpret behavior patterns, or historians understand events. When teachers ground their instruction in the literacy of their discipline, they are initiating their students into ways of thinking, working, and seeing—and, by doing this, treating them as apprentices to a field that teacher has devoted their life to understanding. As Lent writes, quoting a teacher, "The only knowledge that will stick, that will be available to build on next month or next year (or in college), is knowledge that a student has worked to understand" (p. 200).

What to Do

To understand what these disciplinary literacies are and how to make them the focus of your own class, read the following questions and, in the space on the next page, write your answers as they apply to the subjects and classes you teach:

- What best describes the discipline you teach?

- What are the essential "habits of thinking" and ways of working practiced by those in your field?

- What are the core creative and critical thinking skills people in your discipline use to identify and solve discipline-specific problems?

- How do practitioners within your discipline work, in both self-directed and collaborative ways, as they plan, share, and assess learning within that discipline?

- How do people in your field "find meaning as it relates to the discipline as they wrestle with project plans, disciplinary principles, and demonstrations of learning" (p. 7)?

- How do experts in your field read, write, and speak in the context of their work?

What to Remember

Students are learning the literacies of a specific discipline when they are "acting as apprentices in a real-world setting, constructing and applying knowledge, learning from each other, and asking for help when needed" (p. 199), just as anyone in that field—of history, government, literary studies, biology—would in the context of their work.

Equity and Access Check

____ I define and clarify for all students what I am teaching them to do, why, and how they will learn and demonstrate that learning.

____ I provide models and demonstrate for students what the specific literacy skills look like.

____ I monitor the progress and understanding of students who are likely to struggle with what I am teaching or the way I am teaching and assessing their performance.

____ I provide a range of interventions--individual, small group, whole class--based on my observations and the data I collect from their performance on an assignment or assessment.

____ I ensure that my lessons are designed to accommodate any learning difficulties or language needs students may have and check with relevant colleagues for suggested strategies to use.

NOTES

MONTH 5

YEAR

LOOKING AHEAD: What is the most important outcome to accomplish by the end of the month—and why?

Notes/Events	Focus 1: What and Why?	Focus 2: What and Why?	Focus 3: What and Why?
	What is your focus and why?	What is your focus and why?	What is your focus and why?

	Focus 1: When and What?	Focus 2: When and What?	Focus 3: When and What?
	When do you work on it and what do you do?	When do you work on it and what do you do?	When do you work on it and what do you do?

The Six Commitments

1. I am committed to the success and well-being of all my students and to their learning.
2. I know my subject and how to teach it so that all my students will learn, remember, and enjoy it.
3. I am responsible for designing, teaching, and assessing the lessons and learning of all my students.
4. I consider equity and access when designing, teaching, and assessing my lessons and students' learning.
5. I reflect on, analyze, and refine my teaching based on feedback from multiple sources.
6. I participate in and contribute to my learning community at school and the profession at large.

Reflect on the one commitment you made the greatest progress on or struggled with the most this month.

HABIT TRACKER DIRECTIONS: List specific **actions** in the left column that will help you develop and maintain healthy habits. Indicate your daily results with a code that works for you. At least some of these habits should be directly related to your three key areas in which you are trying to improve or achieve some specific result this year. Go to jamesclear.com/habit-tracker for more information about tracking your habits.

Habits	1	2	3	4	5	6	7	8	9	10	11	12	13	14	15	16	17	18	19	20	21	22	23	24	25	26	27	28	29	30	31

PROFESSIONAL: Review and reflect on your weekly self-evaluations for the past month.	**PERSONAL:** Review and reflect on your weekly self-evaluations for the past month.	**KIDS:** Check In/Check On

MONTH 5

MANAGING YOUR KIDS, CLASSROOM, AND CURRICULUM | **FOCUS: ENGAGEMENT**

5. Increase **engagement** through instructional approaches, curriculum, and experiences that are academically, socially, culturally, and emotionally challenging and relevant.

One of the primary reasons for classroom management problems is that students are not engaged (in-person or online). As the saying goes: If students do not know the WHY they will not care about the WHAT or HOW. In short, effective teachers get students "busily engaged in important, interesting, and challenging work" (Lemov, 2015, p. 346). Hammond (2014) says that the Academic Mindset Cycle "begins with the belief that learning is relevant and is worth paying attention to," at which point "the brain is captured by positive emotion, physical energy, curiosity, or a puzzle signaling the brain to engage" (p. 111). Fisher, Frey, and Quaglia (2018) distinguish between three types of engagement: behavioral (fundamental academic behaviors, such as attending, participating, and completing assignments), cognitive (how much students care about and invest in learning content or completing assignments), and emotional (how students feel about their school community and the people who teach or learn alongside them) (p. 134).

Assess yourself by answering T (True), F (False), S (Sometimes)

____ I design lessons that allow for student voice and choice.

____ I plan my lessons so that they leave no "dead time."

____ I use a range of instructional materials, approaches, and configurations designed to keep students engaged.

____ I create learning experiences that connect to students' interests, culture, experiences, and priorities.

____ I use technology to engage and support but also challenge students to collaborate and create.

____ I evaluate the lessons and units I design to be sure that all students, including those with special needs or those who are learning English, will be able to engage with and be engaged by any activities or assignments the class is doing.

____ I monitor and follow up with those students who are not doing or submitting work, participating, or working with others.

____ I know and make sure that students understand what I am teaching, why, and how they will know if they learned it.

WORK ON: COMMUNICATION
THE IMPORTANCE OF LANGUAGE AND TONE IN THE CLASSROOM

Words have power to build people up or break them down. When teachers use encouraging words and affirm the effort of their students, they are improving the learning experience. Upon hearing those positive words, students will have better self-confidence, they will put forth more effort, and thus they will perform better academically. On the other hand, among students who hear their teachers, parents, or peers speak negatively about them, self-confidence often plummets. This then decreases their motivation to do the hard work required for learning: thus their ability to succeed is greatly diminished. —Eric Jensen and Liesl McConchie, *Brain-Based Learning: Teaching the Way Students Really Learn*

	MONTH 5		YEAR
NOTES	Monday	Tuesday	Wednesday

CHECK IN • CHECK UP • CHECK OUT

Visit Ryan Holiday's website (ryanholiday.net) to learn from the Stoic philosophers or sign up for his *Daily Stoic* newsletter (dailystoic.com) that is brief and full of practical wisdom. I read it daily and swear by it.

MONTH 5

Thursday	Friday	Saturday	Sunday

LOOKING BACK: END OF THE SEMESTER TWO-WAY REFLECTION
PROFESSIONAL AND PERSONAL

Directions: Pause here at the end of the semester to review and reflect on how things are going for you professionally and personally. As you to look back over the past semester, evaluate what has and has not gone well for you as a teacher, as a team, and as a person with your many obligations outside the classroom.

PROFESSIONAL The Six Commitments	TEAM The Six Characteristics	PERSONAL The Six Categories of Well-Being
1. **Success and Well-Being**: I am committed to the success and well-being of all my students and to their learning. 2. **Subject Matter Knowledge**: I know my subject and how to teach it so that all my students will learn, remember, and enjoy it. 3. **Designing, Teaching, Assessing**: I am responsible for designing, teaching, and assessing the lessons and learning of all my students. 4. **Equity and Access**: I consider equity and access when designing, teaching, and assessing my lessons and students' learning. 5. **Feedback on Teaching**: I reflect on, analyze, and refine my teaching based on feedback from multiple sources. 6. **Professional Community**: I participate in and contribute to my learning community at school and the profession at large.	1. **Structural Conditions**: How well do our schedules and systems ensure effective collaboration and reduce isolation? 2. **Supportive Relational Conditions**: How much do we trust and respect each other and feel we can speak honestly about our work? 3. **Shared Values and Vision**: To what extent do we share the same goal, vision, and beliefs about student learning and our impact on it? 4. **Intentional Collective Learning**: How well do we share our knowledge, practices, skills, and strategies about what impacts learning? 5. **Peers Supporting Peers**: To what extent and in what ways do the members of our team celebrate and support each other? 6. **Shared and Supportive Leadership**: How do we share power, authority, and decision making? How is our relationship with the leaders and administrators?	1. **Contentment**: I felt good about things in general this semester. 2. **Connection**: I felt connected to my friends, family, community, and interests this semester. 3. **Condition**: I felt physically, mentally, and spiritually/existentially healthy this semester. 4. **Commitments**: I met all of my obligations to myself and others this semester. 5. **Control**: I felt like I was in control of my life and its demands this semester. 6. **Concerns**: My three greatest concerns this semester were:

LOOKING AHEAD: END OF THE SEMESTER TWO-WAY REFLECTION
PROFESSIONAL AND PERSONAL

Directions: As you think ahead to next semester, consider how you would like things to change for you professionally and personally. Keep in mind what has and has not worked for you as a teacher, a team, and a person this semester. What small changes can you make to improve things a little bit each day when you come back in January?

PROFESSIONAL The Six Commitments	TEAM The Six Characteristics	PERSONAL The Six Categories of Well-Being
1. **Success and Well-Being**: I am committed to the success and well-being of all my students and to their learning. 2. **Subject Matter Knowledge**: I know my subject and how to teach it so that all my students will learn, remember, and enjoy it. 3. **Designing, Teaching, Assessing**: I am responsible for designing, teaching, and assessing the lessons and learning of all my students. 4. **Equity and Access**: I consider equity and access when designing, teaching, and assessing my lessons and students' learning. 5. **Feedback on Teaching**: I reflect on, analyze, and refine my teaching based on feedback from multiple sources. 6. **Professional Community**: I participate in and contribute to my learning community at school and the profession at large.	1. **Structural Conditions**: How well do our schedules and systems ensure effective collaboration and reduce isolation? 2. **Supportive Relational Conditions**: How much do we trust and respect each other and feel we can speak honestly about our work? 3. **Shared Values and Vision**: To what extent do we share the same goal, vision, and beliefs about student learning and our impact on it? 4. **Intentional Collective Learning**: How well do we share our knowledge, practices, skills, and strategies about what impacts learning? 5. **Peers Supporting Peers**: To what extent and in what ways do the members of our team celebrate and support each other? 6. **Shared and Supportive Leadership**: How do we share power, authority, and decision making? How is our relationship with the leaders and administrators?	1. **Contentment**: I feel optimistic and encouraged about next semester. 2. **Connection**: How can I stay or be more connected to my friends, family, community, and interests next semester? 3. **Condition**: I have a plan to help me be physically, mentally, and spiritually/existentially healthy next semester. 4. **Commitments**: I am confident that I can meet my obligations to myself and others during the next semester. 5. **Control**: I am confident I will feel a degree of control over my life and its demands next semester. 6. **Concerns**: My three greatest concerns for next semester are: _____ _____ _____

Courageous Conversations About Race: A Field Guide for Achieving Equity in Schools (2015)
Glenn Singleton

> "As schools engage in open and honest dialogue about racial achievement disparities, they can effectively address the obstacles to success that exist for all students" (p. 26).

Singleton provides a protocol he calls Courageous Conversation that teachers can use to "engage, sustain, and deepen the conversation about race in their schools" (p. 4). He defines Courageous Conversation as "the agreements, conditions, and compass to engage, sustain, and deepen interracial dialogue about race in order to examine schooling and improve student achievement" (p. 26). Singleton's premise is that race "plays a primary role in sustaining if not widening the omnipresent achievement gaps" (p. 4) in schools in large part because people do not know how to have the honest conversations necessary to initiate and sustain the changes. Central to such conversations is trust and the role it plays in having and sustaining such conversations.

Singleton poses three essential questions teachers must consider when addressing the racial achievement gap (p. 11):

1. What is it that educators should know and be able to do to narrow the racial achievement gap?

2. How will educators know when they are experiencing success in their efforts to narrow the racial achievement gap?

3. What do educators do as they discover what they don't yet know and are not yet able to do to eliminate the racial achievement gap?

Singleton also asks that teachers practice the Four Agreements: (1) stay engaged, (2) speak your truth, (3) experience discomfort, and (4) expect and accept nonclosure (p. 27).

The purpose of a Courageous Conversation is to engage those who won't talk; sustain the conversation when it gets uncomfortable or diverted; and deepen the conversation to the point where authentic understanding and meaningful actions occur. While the Four Agreements define the process, the Six Conditions describe the content and progression of the Courageous Conversation (p. 28):

(1) Establish a racial context that is personal, local, and immediate.

(2) Isolate race while acknowledging the broader scope of diversity and the variety of factors that contribute to a racialized problem.

(3) Develop understanding of race as a social/political construction of knowledge and engage multiple racial perspectives to surface critical understanding.

(4) Monitor the parameters of the conversation by being explicit and intentional about the number of participants, prompts for discussion, and time allotted for listening, speaking, and reflecting.

(5) Establish agreement around a working definition of race, one that is clearly differentiated from ethnicity and nationality.

(6) Examine the presence and role of whiteness and its impact on the conversation and the problem being addressed.

What to Do

Early in the book, Singleton describes a high school that has consistently ranked among the top schools in its state in every subject area. After disaggregating their performance data, however, they discovered that students of color were scoring far below white and Asian students on these same assessments. So, they began a Courageous Conversation with all stakeholders which they have sustained. Consider gathering performance data for your own classes, your department, or the whole school. Then, after examining it, use these three questions to guide your reflection on the opposite page: (1) Why do racial gaps exist? (2) What is the origin of the racial gaps? (3) What factors have allowed these gaps to persist for so many years?

What to Remember

Singleton identifies four primary ways that people respond to racial information, events, and issues: emotional, intellectual, moral, and relational (how we act in such situations). Teachers need the structures, agreements, and essential conditions that will allow them to engage in and sustain the Courageous Conversation they need to have if they are to help all students succeed in school and life. Singleton identifies Three Ps as central to racial equity leadership: "Emboldened with passion, enabled with practice, and strengthened by persistence, we can create schools in which all students achieve at higher levels, achievement gaps are narrowed, and the racial predictability and disproportionality of high and low student achievement are eliminated" (p. 21).

Equity and Access Check

____ I define and clarify for all my students what I am teaching, why I am teaching it, how I will teach them, and how they will be assessed and by what criteria.

____ I examine the texts, tasks, techniques, and tests for any obstacles to the success of all students specifically having to do with race. If I discover such obstacles, I analyze and address them, using the ideas outlined earlier as a guide.

____ I gather data about student performance in my class and monitor the progress and understanding of all students but look specifically at the scores of students of color to identify and address possible inequities, obstacles, or instructional needs.

____ I consider and choose from a range of interventions and strategies to help identify problems, solutions, and questions for me, our department, team, or school to consider as part of our Courageous Conversation. If needed, we invite facilitators to help us have these conversations.

NOTES

MONTH 6

YEAR

LOOKING AHEAD: What is the most important outcome to accomplish by the end of the month—and why?

Notes/Events	Focus 1: What and Why?	Focus 2: What and Why?	Focus 3: What and Why?
	What is your focus and why?	What is your focus and why?	What is your focus and why?
	Focus 1: When and What?	**Focus 2: When and What?**	**Focus 3: When and What?**
	When do you work on it and what do you do?	When do you work on it and what do you do?	When do you work on it and what do you do?

MONTH 6

The Six Commitments

1. I am committed to the success and well-being of all my students and to their learning.
2. I know my subject and how to teach it so that all my students will learn, remember, and enjoy it.
3. I am responsible for designing, teaching, and assessing the lessons and learning of all my students.
4. I consider equity and access when designing, teaching, and assessing my lessons and students' learning.
5. I reflect on, analyze, and refine my teaching based on feedback from multiple sources.
6. I participate in and contribute to my learning community at school and the profession at large.

Reflect on the one commitment you made the greatest progress on or struggled with the most this month.

HABIT TRACKER DIRECTIONS: List specific **actions** in the left column that will help you develop and maintain healthy habits. Indicate your daily results with a code that works for you. At least some of these habits should be directly related to your three key areas in which you are trying to improve or achieve some specific result this year. Go to jamesclear.com/habit-tracker for more information about tracking your habits.

HABITS	1	2	3	4	5	6	7	8	9	10	11	12	13	14	15	16	17	18	19	20	21	22	23	24	25	26	27	28	29	30	31

LOOKING BACK: What did I do just a little bit better this month? How did I do just a little bit better day by day this month?

PROFESSIONAL: Review and reflect on your weekly self-evaluations for the past month.	**PERSONAL:** Review and reflect on your weekly self-evaluations for the past month.	**KIDS**: Check In/Check On

---

MANAGING YOUR KIDS, CLASSROOM, AND CURRICULUM

6. *Recognize and monitor your own **attitudes, assumptions, biases, and values** and how they can affect the way you teach, speak to, respond to, or think about your students.*

What This Means and Why It Matters

CRM (Classroom Management) is not about controlling students or achieving dominance over them; rather, it is about ensuring that all students have equitable opportunities to learn and succeed in the class. The lenses through which we view our students determine how we interpret what they do and say. So, if we are not aware of our own lenses, we may misinterpret students' behaviors or performance unfairly. Such misunderstanding is further avoided by maintaining "emotional objectivity" (Marzano et al., 2003, p. 73) and taking time to monitor our own attitudes about and responses to specific students or situations. Such monitoring can reveal or help us to counter the biases or attitudes that may be unknowingly shaping our actions. Hammond (2014) argues that this process of self-awareness begins with "intention [as] the starting point for preparing yourself for improving your culturally responsive teaching practice" (p. 55). This process asks teachers to complete three "internal tasks": (1) identify your cultural frame of reference, (2) widen your cultural aperture, and (3) identify your key triggers (p. 56). We might summarize much of the thinking for this item with Maya Angelou's observation that "people will forget what you said, people will forget what you did, but people will never forget how you made them feel."

FOCUS: ATTITUDES, ASSUMPTIONS, BIASES, AND VALUES

Assess yourself by answering T (True), F (False), S (Sometimes)

____ I evaluate and reflect on my own biases and assumptions periodically using tools such as Project Implicit or the Cultural Proficiency Receptivity Scale.

____ I am honest with myself about my own attitudes, assumptions, biases, and values and how they influence my teaching and my interactions with students.

____ I gather feedback about my interactions with students (how I speak, what I say, whom I call on) from students, colleagues, or video recording.

____ I set aside time on a regular basis to conduct empathy interviews using the tool from *Street Data* (Safir and Dugan, 2021) and adjust my practice, curriculum, or environment as needed based on what students say.

____ I gather information on referrals, detentions, suspensions, or other disciplinary actions in my class and examine it for any patterns that suggest how I can improve.

____ I make a deliberate effort with all my students to avoid making any assumptions about their character or abilities based on their appearance, handwriting, race, culture, style of dress, way they speak, or other such elements.

WORK ON: GRADING
THE PLACE AND PURPOSE OF GRADING IN YOUR CLASS CULTURE AND CURRICULUM

Grading practices are a mirror not just to students, but to us, their teachers. Each teacher's grading choices—whether to offer students redemption or a single chance, whether to reward students or punish them based on prior educational experiences or environment, to invite biases or restrain them, to describe in a grade only what students know or to include how they behave, to make students dependent on our judgment or empower them to self-assess and connect their behavior to their achievement—all of those choices reflect who that teacher is and what she believes in. —Joe Feldman, *Grading for Equity*

	MONTH 6		YEAR
Notes	**Monday**	**Tuesday**	**Wednesday**

CHECK IN • CHECK UP • CHECK OUT

Visit Gretchen Rubin's website (gretchenrubin .com) to enjoy the many useful resources she offers as part of her Happiness Project work. She puts out a wonderful weekly newsletter that I recommend.

Thursday	Friday	Saturday	Sunday

MONTH 8

Equity by Design: Delivering on the Power and Promise of UDL (2021)
Mirko Chardin and Katie Novak

"We have the authority and privilege to design learning
environments that empower students to become motivated,
purposeful, resourceful, and strategic or expert learners, which
is the goal of Universal Design for Learning (UDL)" (p. 65).

Chardin and Novak anchor their book in the principles of Universal Design for Learning (UDL), which is based on three guiding principles intended to help teachers offer students multiple ways to personalize their learning experience. In short, students should be provided (1) multiple means of engagement, (2) multiple means of representation, and (3) multiple means of action and expression. The authors insist that UDL "eliminates barriers to learning" in ways that a "one-size-fits-all" teacher-designed curriculum cannot; moreover, such "barriers" weaken equity in two ways: they limit access to learning and undermine engagement (p. 4).

Two essential ingredients—choice and voice—run throughout their examination of UDL and how teachers can apply these principles. The authors ask, "How often, in your learning environment, do all students truly have choice and voice?" (p. 5). See https://udlguidelines.cast.org/ for more information on UDL.

What to Do

In the space provided on the next page, reflect on and respond to the following questions from the chapter "Universal Design as an Instrument of Change" (p. 8) in *Equity by Design*. Use your responses to have the courageous conversation you need to have with yourself, your team, department, school, or district:

- What is our desired impact?
- What do we want our students to become?
- What world, society, and/or time period are we preparing them for?
- What does it look, feel, and sound like when we are successful?
- What role do we play in student success?
- How have we engaged in courageous conversations?
- How do we acknowledge and celebrate differences?
- Do all members of our school community feel safe, seen, and heard?
- Does our work validate the lives and experiences of folks from different backgrounds and/or identities?

What to Remember

Chardin and Novak highlight six "critical signposts in the journey" of aligning our instructional practice to UDL (p. 9):

(1) Identify the barriers (of any type) that prevent instruction and learning for all students.

(2) Embrace variability that is inherent in all humans.

(3) Reflect on our biases and the ways these might undermine teaching and learning.

(4) Expect discomfort when engaging in the necessary conversations.

(5) Amplify student voice by making room for students to speak, contribute, and participate.

(6) Take action by having the courage to examine, revise, and make room for the principles of UDL.

Equity and Access Check

_____ I examine any resources, materials, or software applications I use to identify any obstacles that would prevent all my students from learning the intended lesson or engaging in an assignment or activity.

_____ I make sure that students have meaningful opportunities for choice and voice on assignments so as to increase engagement.

_____ I provide students a range of ways to demonstrate their learning on a given assignment.

_____ I provide a range of interventions, including working with them individually or within a small group, to ensure they have the skills and knowledge needed to succeed on an assignment.

_____ I seek out colleagues who have had success with a specific student or know techniques that would be helpful for one or more students in my class who are struggling in a specific area.

_____ I provide student examples or demonstrate myself what a successful performance on a given assignment looks like and how they can accomplish such an outcome.

NOTES

MONTH 7

YEAR

LOOKING AHEAD: What is the most important outcome to accomplish by the end of the month—and why?

MONTH /

Notes/Events	Focus 1: What and Why?	Focus 2: What and Why?	Focus 3: What and Why?
	What is your focus and why?	What is your focus and why?	What is your focus and why?

	Focus 1: When and What?	Focus 2: When and What?	Focus 3: When and What?
	When do you work on it and what do you do?	When do you work on it and what do you do?	When do you work on it and what do you do?

The Six Commitments

1. I am committed to the success and well-being of all my students and to their learning.
2. I know my subject and how to teach it so that all my students will learn, remember, and enjoy it.
3. I am responsible for designing, teaching, and assessing the lessons and learning of all my students.
4. I consider equity and access when designing, teaching, and assessing my lessons and students' learning.
5. I reflect on, analyze, and refine my teaching based on feedback from multiple sources.
6. I participate in and contribute to my learning community at school and the profession at large.

Reflect on the one commitment you made the greatest progress on or struggled with the most this month.

HABIT TRACKER DIRECTIONS: List specific **actions** in the left column that will help you develop and maintain healthy habits. Indicate your daily results with a code that works for you. At least some of these habits should be directly related to your three key areas in which you are trying to improve or achieve some specific result this year. Go to jamesclear.com/habit-tracker for more information about tracking your habits.

HABITS	1	2	3	4	5	6	7	8	9	10	11	12	13	14	15	16	17	18	19	20	21	22	23	24	25	26	27	28	29	30	31

LOOKING BACK: What did I do just a little bit better this month? How did I do just a little bit better day by day this month?

PROFESSIONAL: Review and reflect on your weekly self-evaluations for the past month.	**PERSONAL:** Review and reflect on your weekly self-evaluations for the past month.	**KIDS:** Check In/Check On

MANAGING YOUR KIDS, CLASSROOM, AND CURRICULUM

FOCUS: INDEPENDENCE

7. *Cultivate independence* in students so that they can use their social and emotional intelligence to manage themselves and their relationships with others.

What This Means and Why It Matters

One of the primary aims of education is to learn how to work with other people in different situations so that our students can be independent.

This means they need to learn how to ask for and offer help, whether working alone or with others, in-class or online. Marzano et al. (2003) refer to "self- monitoring and control techniques" (p. 78) through which the teacher shows students how to observe, record, and compare their actions with established criteria appropriate to the task. For example, students could keep track of the number of times they contribute to a class discussion or document and reflect on what they contribute to a group. A variation on such self-monitoring would be what Marzano et al. call "cognitively based strategies" (p. 85), which involve examining what one did, thought, or felt during an activity, assignment, or other situation that offered ways to think about what, how, and why they said what they did. Hannigan and Hannigan (2021) identify the following social and emotional learning (SEL) competencies as essential for students to master: relationship skills, responsible decision making, social awareness, self-management, and self-awareness (p. 120). To these SEL skills, Daniels and Steineke (2014) add "the missing link" they call "social-academic skills," which they argue are essential for best practice instruction and can only be developed "in a flexible, decentralized classroom where kids take action in a variety of configurations, assume responsibility, work with pride, hold themselves accountable, and support one another" (p. 6).

Assess yourself by answering T (True), F (False), S (Sometimes)

____ I have students monitor, evaluate, and reflect on their behavior, work habits, and participation to help them identify what they do well and what they can improve.

____ I ask myself when designing an activity, assignment, or assessment if there is a way for students to take responsibility or have a meaningful choice.

____ I apply the gradual release of responsibility model when designing lessons or teaching my students.

____ I ask students to self-assess their work or performance according to criteria we discuss or I provide, then review the reasons for their score and how they can improve.

____ I ask students to use various self-management strategies to keep track of their standing, assignments, and progress on projects, whether working in-class or online, on their own or with others.

____ I expect and teach students how to advocate for what they need to succeed in a social or academic situation using certain strategies or language structures to ask for help.

____ I help students develop impulse-control strategies for managing their cell phone use and online behavior.

WORK ON: LEARNING TRANSFER
THE CHALLENGE OF UNDERSTANDING AND RETAINING WHAT THEY LEARN

Students bring preconceived notions and misunderstandings to learning experiences all the time. Unless we confront these misconceptions head on, students will learn what we want them to learn, and at the end of the unit forget it and go back to believing what they originally thought. A simple strategy to use throughout the entire unit is "at first I thought . . ., but now I think . . ." This strategy should be used as students move through [the] acquire, connect, and transfer phases of learning. . . . Imagine how much more confident students might feel and the quality of the thought that would result if they made a habit of monitoring their learning in all classes. —Julie Stern, Krista Ferraro, Kayla Duncan, and Trevor Aleo, *Learning that Transfers: Designing Curriculum for a Changing World*

MONTH 7 — YEAR

Notes	Monday	Tuesday	Wednesday

CHECK IN • CHECK UP • CHECK OUT

Visit Daniel Pink's website (www.danpink.com) to learn about when we should do everything from having meetings to drinking coffee, exercising, and taking naps.

Thursday	Friday	Saturday	Sunday

MONTH 7

SEL from a Distance: Tools and Processes for Anytime, Anywhere (2021)
Jessica Djabrayan Hannigan and John E. Hannigan

> "Social and emotional learning (SEL) is not a thing to do. It is the way of being—all day every day—in any setting." (p. 33)

The authors define SEL this way: "social and emotional learning enhances students' capacity to integrate skills, attitudes, and behaviors to deal effectively and ethically with daily tasks and challenges" (p. 10).

Though they list many important statistics, perhaps this one best captures the SEL needs of our times: one in five children has mental health challenges (p. 4). Their essential claim is that "SEL is not just a curriculum . . . [but] the intentional identification, teaching, modeling, and reinforcement of the necessary SEL skills for success in school and life" (p. 117). Though their focus is on the SEL skills of students, one cannot read the book without realizing that these same skills are just as necessary for teachers if they are to be successful and well themselves.

What to Do

Hannigan and Hannigan identify and organize their book around Five Core SEL Competencies— Relationship Skills, Responsible Decision Making, Social Awareness, Self-Management, and Self- Awareness (p. 10)—and they present these competencies within the context of a three-stage implementation framework: Phase 1: Prioritize, Phase 2: Mastery, and Phase 3: SEL Teaching Process.

This book offers a wealth of practical applications. Here is one activity you can use for a specific student, your own classes, or your PLC, department, or school. Rank each of the following SEL competencies in terms of their priority (1 = highest priority and 5 = lowest priority).

____ **Relationship Skills:** communication, social engagement, relationship building, teamwork

____ **Responsible Decision Making:** identifying problems, analyzing situations, solving problems, evaluation, reflecting, ethical responsibility

____ **Social Awareness:** perspective taking, empathy, appreciating diversity, respect from others

____ **Self-Management:** impulse control, stress management, self-discipline, self-motivation, goal setting, organizational skills

____ **Self-Awareness:** identifying emotions, accurate self-perception, recognizing strengths, self- confidence, self-efficacy

Highest priority SEL competency: _____

What to Remember

As Hannigan and Hannigan emphasize, SEL skills are teachable and essential if students are to learn, remember, and do what we teach. The Five Core SEL Competencies listed above are, they emphasize, best developed through their SEL Teaching Process: (1) identify the most urgent SEL competencies, (2) teach the relevant SEL competency skill(s) explicitly, (3) model the skills daily through actions and examples, and (4) reinforce the skill(s) taught daily and whenever possible.

Equity and Access Check

____ I define and clarify for all students the SEL skills and principles I am teaching, why they are important, how I will teach them, and how they will know they have learned them.

____ I provide models and demonstrate for students what the specific SEL skills look like.

____ I monitor the progress and understanding of students who struggle to learn or whose behaviors would undermine the lesson or the learning environment of the class.

____ I provide a range of interventions, including meetings with parents, counselors, or other support team members to understand the student's behavior and help them learn the lesson.

____ I ensure that my lessons are designed to accommodate any learning difficulties or language needs students may have and check with relevant colleagues for suggested strategies to use.

____ I create opportunities for students to work with and get to know a wide range of students in the classroom to ensure they learn and use the SEL skills that are a vital part of the class.

NOTES

MONTH 8

YEAR

LOOKING AHEAD: What is the most important outcome to accomplish by the end of the month—and why?

Notes/Events	Focus 1: What and Why?	Focus 2: What and Why?	Focus 3: What and Why?
	What is your focus and why?	What is your focus and why?	What is your focus and why?

	Focus 1: When and What?	Focus 2: When and What?	Focus 3: When and What?
	When do you work on it and what do you do?	When do you work on it and what do you do?	When do you work on it and what do you do?

The Six Commitments

1. I am committed to the success and well-being of all my students and to their learning.
2. I know my subject and how to teach it so that all my students will learn, remember, and enjoy it.
3. I am responsible for designing, teaching, and assessing the lessons and learning of all my students.
4. I consider equity and access when designing, teaching, and assessing my lessons and students' learning.
5. I reflect on, analyze, and refine my teaching based on feedback from multiple sources.
6. I participate in and contribute to my learning community at school and the profession at large.

Reflect on the one commitment you made the greatest progress on or struggled with the most this month.

HABIT TRACKER DIRECTIONS: List specific **actions** in the left column that will help you develop and maintain healthy habits. Indicate your daily results with a code that works for you. At least some of these habits should be directly related to your three key areas in which you are trying to improve or achieve some specific result this year. Go to jamesclear.com/habit-tracker for more information about tracking your habits.

HABITS	1	2	3	4	5	6	7	8	9	10	11	12	13	14	15	16	17	18	19	20	21	22	23	24	25	26	27	28	29	30	31

PROFESSIONAL: Review and reflect on your weekly self-evaluations for the past month.	**PERSONAL:** Review and reflect on your weekly self-evaluations for the past month.	**KIDS:** Check In/Check On

MANAGING YOUR KIDS, CLASSROOM, AND CURRICULUM

FOCUS: NECESSARY CONDITIONS

*8. Provide the **necessary conditions** for students to succeed on all assignments in-class and online, whether working individually or in groups.*

What This Means and Why It Matters

One condition that is often neglected and yet is essential for us to provide classroom management that is fair, consistent, and effective is our own well-being. As Marzano (2003) writes, this "strategy for maintaining a healthy emotional objectivity has nothing to do with students. Rather it has to do with taking care of your own emotional health" (p. 74). Curwin and Mendler (1988) explain the benefits of taking care of ourselves: "We have stated time and time again that it is critical for you not to carry anger, resentment, and other hostile feelings once a discipline situation is over. If you are angry with a student from an incident that happened the day before, you might enter a power struggle just to flex your muscles and show who is boss. Don't. Start fresh each day" (p. 105). Hammond (2014) asks teachers to give "dependent learners the basic tools for independent living" (p. 98). These include providing students "[1] kid-friendly vocabulary for talking about their learning moves . . ., [2] checklists to help [students] hone their decision-making skills during learning and focus their attention during data analysis . . ., [3] tools for tracking their own progress toward learning targets . . ., [4] easily accessible space to store their data . . ., [5] regular time to process their data . . ., [6] practice engaging in metacognitive conversations about their learning moves and cognitive strategy as it relates to their learning . . ., [7] a clear process for reflecting on and acting on teacher or peer feedback" (pp. 100–101).

Assess yourself by answering T (True), F (False), S (Sometimes)

_____ I ensure that all students have access to and know how to use any tools, technology, materials, or resources they must have to do assignments in-class or online, including Wi-Fi, computers, calculators, and software applications.

_____ I check and monitor to be sure students with 504 or IEP plans, or any other learning needs, have the knowledge, skills, or resources they need to do an assignment or activity in-class or online.

_____ I make sure every student can see and hear as needed to learn from where they are seated; also, I evaluate where vulnerable students or those with special needs sit to make sure they do not feel marginalized, unsafe, or otherwise prevented from learning.

_____ I constantly evaluate and adjust as needed the learning environment in-class and online to remove any potential distractions or other variables that would impede learning.

_____ I do not call out or "cold call" students who would be embarrassed or have a panic attack.

_____ I show or express my gratitude and enthusiasm for students' contributions, efforts, and progress.

_____ I monitor and solicit students' feedback about how known, valued, respected, and safe they feel in my class and online.

WORK ON: CLASSROOM CULTURE
THE IMPORTANCE OF MAKING EVERYONE FEEL SAFE, WELCOME, AND CAPABLE

Fish Out of Water are people who are different because they do not know or meet the cultural expectations of their environments effectively. Many of these outsiders are simply people who don't know how to code switch. Others get targeted because they belong to groups that are unacceptable to the dominant culture; they are the outsiders who are pushed to the margins or who choose to walk there to avoid predators. In any organization or pond there are people on the margins, who may be invisible and voiceless to those who have greater influence in the environment. —Kikanza Nuri-Robins and Lewis Bundy, *Fish Out of Water: Mentoring, Managing, and Self-Monitoring People Who Don't Fit In*

	MONTH 8	YEAR	
NOTES	**Monday**	**Tuesday**	**Wednesday**

CHECK IN • CHECK UP • CHECK OUT

Visit Edutopia (edutopia. org/topic/teacher-wellness) to enjoy the many helpful resources they offer to help teachers be and STAY well.

MONTH 8

Thursday	Friday	Saturday	Sunday

MONTH 8

Better Conversations: Coaching Ourselves and Each Other to Be More Credible, Caring, and Connected (2016)
Jim Knight

> "When teachers are clearer, ask better questions, and foster dialogue, their students learn more" (p. 2).

In this thoughtful book, Knight, who has devoted much of his career to studying how we teach, seeks to help teachers have better conversations about their work, their students, and their schools with the people at the heart of those conversations: teachers themselves, their colleagues, their students, and their parents. As Knight argues, we all need these conversations because we are all "radically broken," by which he means that too many of us live in isolation from those we live, work, and learn with. Though we have more ways to connect than ever before, this idea of being radically broken undermines the feeling of "unity [which] is our natural state." It is through better conversations that Knight believes we can "heal that radical brokenness and restore unity." As he states early on, "Our schools are only as good as the conversations within them" (p. 4).

But what are these better conversations? They are conversations in which one should "position the person I'm speaking with as a full partner rather than an 'audience.'" Such conversations "are grounded in both a set of beliefs and a collection of habits that are the embodiment of those beliefs." Better conversations, Knight emphasizes, "can happen anywhere in a school: teacher to teacher, coach to coach, principal to teacher, teacher to student, student to student, and teacher to parent" (p. 6).

Knight identifies two key elements of the kind of better conversations he is urging us to foster, participate in, and help to sustain: beliefs and habits. Beliefs "give shape to who we are and what we do" (p. 9) as individuals, groups, and organizations. Habits are the other half of this combination, because, as Knight asserts, "the best way to imagine communication practices is as a collection of habits" (p. 10). More specifically, ineffective habits we must replace with effective communication habits.

What to Do

Certainly, Knight's entire book, *Better Conversations*, warrants your full attention, but for now consider these habits and beliefs that serve as the foundation for his vision of a class, team, or school that seeks common ground and, through these habits and beliefs, builds trust and cultivates empathy:

- **The Better Conversations Habits:** (1) Demonstrating Empathy, (2) Listening with Empathy, (3) Fostering Dialogue, (4) Asking Better Questions, (5) Making Emotional Connections, (6) Being a Witness to the Good, (7) Finding Common Ground, (8) Controlling Toxic Emotions, (9) Redirecting Toxic Conversations, (10) Building Trust

- **The Better Conversations Beliefs:** (1) I see conversation partners as equals, (2) I want to hear what others have to say, (3) I believe people should have a lot of autonomy, (4) I don't judge others, (5) Conversation should be back and forth, (6) Conversation should be life-giving

After choosing one habit and one belief that you know would improve the conversations within your class, on your team, in your department, or across the entire school, write about what you think each of your selections means and how each one applies to your situation. Consider its causes and effects, as well as its implications for all involved. Resist the urge to complain or blame; instead, focus on why these habits and beliefs are important and how you might use them to improve your conversations with colleagues, students, and parents.

What to Remember

We can always do better and be better—better teachers, leaders, facilitators, collaborators, and so on. Knight's work asks us to pay attention, to observe ourselves and others, to study what is and is not working, then have the conversations with ourselves, our students, or our colleagues about what our students need most from us. This way, as Knight writes, we can have the "healthy conversations and dialogue [that] should leave us feeling better about life and our lives in particular" (p. 4).

Equity and Access Check

____ I define and clarify for whomever I am engaging in a conversation—student, colleague, or other stakeholder—what we are discussing or I am teaching, and why I am teaching it.

____ I approach conversations with students, colleagues, and stakeholders as opportunities to hear what they have to say, and listen to their ideas, suggestions, and concerns without judgment.

____ I provide a range of interventions and strategies designed to help students, colleagues, or stakeholders participate fully in conversations in or outside of the classroom.

____ I ensure that students, colleagues, and stakeholders feel safe and respected during conversations and that they feel they are able to contribute whatever observations, questions, or topics they deem relevant to the discussion we are having.

____ I am responsible for ensuring the conversations we have are productive and transformative, instead of toxic or otherwise counterproductive for those involved.

NOTES

WORK WELL: PREPARE FOR THE MONTH AHEAD

MONTH 9

YEAR

	LOOKING AHEAD: What is the most important outcome to accomplish by the end of the month—and why?

Notes/Events	Focus 1: What and Why?	Focus 2: What and Why?	Focus 3: What and Why?
	What is your focus and why?	What is your focus and why?	What is your focus and why?
	Focus 1: When and What?	**Focus 2: When and What?**	**Focus 3: When and What?**
	When do you work on it and what do you do?	When do you work on it and what do you do?	When do you work on it and what do you do?

The Six Commitments

1. I am committed to the success and well-being of all my students and to their learning.
2. I know my subject and how to teach it so that all my students will learn, remember, and enjoy it.
3. I am responsible for designing, teaching, and assessing the lessons and learning of all my students.
4. I consider equity and access when designing, teaching, and assessing my lessons and students' learning.
5. I reflect on, analyze, and refine my teaching based on feedback from multiple sources.
6. I participate in and contribute to my learning community at school and the profession at large.

Reflect on the one commitment you made the greatest progress on or struggled with the most this month.

HABIT TRACKER DIRECTIONS: List specific **actions** in the left column that will help you develop and maintain healthy habits. Indicate your daily results with a code that works for you. At least some of these habits should be directly related to your three key areas in which you are trying to improve or achieve some specific result this year. Go to jamesclear.com/habit-tracker for more information about tracking your habits.

HABITS	1	2	3	4	5	6	7	8	9	10	11	12	13	14	15	16	17	18	19	20	21	22	23	24	25	26	27	28	29	30	31

LOOKING BACK: What did I do just a little bit better this month? How did I do just a little bit better day by day this month?

PROFESSIONAL: Review and reflect on your weekly self-evaluations for the past month.	PERSONAL: Review and reflect on your weekly self-evaluations for the past month.	Kids: Check In/Check On

MANAGING YOUR KIDS, CLASSROOM, AND CURRICULUM	FOCUS: CONFLICTS AND ESCALATING SITUATIONS

9. *Respond to* **conflicts and escalating situations** *in your classroom with speed, fairness, respect, and a commitment to the safety and well-being of all students.*

What This Means and Why It Matters

Marzano (2003) reports that a balanced approach to discipline (punishment *and* reinforcement) worked best to reduce disruptive behaviors, followed by just reinforcement, only punishment, and no immediate consequence (pp. 28–29). The second type of intervention that shows the strongest results are the verbal and physical actions teachers use to signal that students' behavior is appropriate or inappropriate. Marzano calls such actions "tangible recognition," which he defines as "any type of concrete recognition or reward provided by the teacher" (p. 36). He cautions that "any system of tangible recognition should be accompanied by a thorough discussion of the rationale behind the system . . . [and that] care should be taken to ensure that tangible recognition is not perceived or used as some type of bribe or form of coercion relative to student behavior" (p. 36). All studies single out what Langer (1989) called "situational awareness" (p. 15) and Marzano (2003) labeled "withitness," which amounts to the teacher identifying and intervening immediately to prevent potential crises or conflicts in the classroom (p. 66). Such decisive moments of intervention rely on the teacher exercising what Marzano calls "emotional objectivity" so that they do not exacerbate the situation or cause harm to the teacher-student relationship by misinterpreting a student's cultural actions as behavior problems.

Assess yourself by answering T (True), F (False), S (Sometimes)

____ I constantly monitor the behavior of all students in my classroom, whether in-person or online, working alone or in groups.

____ I intervene immediately but with emotional objectivity when I see potentially disruptive or inappropriate behavior in-class or online.

____ I circulate around the room, noting the status of students' desks, backpacks, computers, phones, and emotional and physical condition for any signs that warrant concern.

____ I evaluate my actions and assumptions for any suggestion of bias, disrespect, or stereotyping based on race, culture, or gender before intervening.

____ I impose a consequence that seems appropriate to the student's behavior (e.g., contacting parents directly, sending student to administrator, speaking to them outside of or keeping them after class) and clarify my rationale.

____ I make changes that avoid or stop conflicts (e.g., change seating assignments, keep student after class, assign detention).

WORK ON: BUILDING TRUST
THE IMPORTANCE OF THE STUDENT-TEACHER RELATIONSHIP IN SCHOOL SUCCESS

Bryk and Schneider also found that relational trust—between teachers and administrators, teachers and teachers, and teachers and parents—has the power to offset external factors that are normally thought to be the primary determinants of a school's capacity to serve students well: "Improvements in academic productivity were less likely in schools with high levels of poverty, racial isolation, and student mobility, but [the researchers] say that a strong correlation between [relational] trust and student achievement remains even after controlling for such factors. —Parker Palmer, *The Courage to Teach*

MONTH 9   YEAR

NOTES	Monday	Tuesday	Wednesday

CHECK IN • CHECK UP • CHECK OUT

Visit the Poetry Foundation website (www. poetryfoundation.org/) to enjoy a poem or sign up for their daily poem newsletter. After all, it *is* National Poetry Month.

Thursday	Friday	Saturday	Sunday

MONTH 9

Quality Questioning: Research-Based Practice to Engage Every Learner, 2nd ed. (2017)
Jackie Acree Walsh and Beth Dankert Sattes

> "Quality questions are the springboards to productive thinking and authentic learning" (p. 10).

In the second edition of *Quality Questioning*, the authors argue that "quality questioning is an organic and dynamic process" (p. 2) that is essential for effective teaching and learning. Citing the influence in recent years of Webb's Depth of Knowledge framework, Hattie's synthesis of thousands of research-based studies, and DuFour's work for professional learning communities, the authors make the case that "quality questioning deepens learning through dialogue and related strategies and that questioning promotes feedback" to both teachers and students (p. 3).

Quality questions, a term they define as "a process informed by research and best practice linked to student achievement," results from "intentional, and ideally collaborative, teacher planning and deliberate, real-time decision-making" (p. 8). Such questions are an integral part of the culture of "learning-oriented classrooms" (p. 18) which the authors describe as "cocreated by students and teachers who value relationships based on mutual trust and respect" (p. 8). In short, quality questioning is a process that springs from the introduction of a question that "focuses attention, stimulates thinking, and results in real learning" (p. 8).

Quality questioning is informed by six core beliefs about teaching and learning: (1) learning requires students to be cognitively and socially engaged as active meaning-makers; (2) questions are vehicles by which students and teachers assess student learning; (3) all students benefit from classroom questions when teachers have explicit expectations about student participation and response; (4) students must have time to think and opportunity to interact to construct connections; (5) teachers can use student responses as feedback to support their next instructional moves; (6) students deepen their learning when they participate in collaborative conversations focused on building academic knowledge and deepening understanding (p. 10). These six core practices are linked to the 6Ps Framework (see the What to Do section that follows).

What to Do

The 6Ps Framework, included below in a general outline for you to consider, offers a series of practices and actions that lead to increased engagement and learning. Each of the following practices influences the other five, all of which culminate in the quality questioning process.

1. Prepare the Question
2. Present the Question
3. Prompt Student Thinking
4. Process Student Responses
5. Polish Questioning Practices
6. Partner With Students

On the page to your left, reflect on your own use of questions in your class, focusing on these six practices and the core beliefs mentioned above. Which of these six practices do you need to work on to improve cognitive and social engagement in your classes? If your use of questions does not include these practices, what do you do instead? For the first practice (Prepare the Question), for example, the authors say teachers should identify a content focus, consider their instructional purpose, determine the desired level of cognitive processing, and fine-tune the wording and syntax of each question (p. 11).

Discuss how that compares with your own question formation process.

What to Remember

Quality questioning is a dynamic process that is at the heart of a learning-centered classroom where the use of such questions to engage students at the highest cognitive levels results in a space where teachers and students share responsibility for intentional learning. As the authors note, summing up the changing relationship between teachers and students that such a shift causes, "Teachers who commit to quality questioning are intentional in changing their own questioning patterns, and they must be explicit with students about expectations for new student roles and responsibilities" (p. 18).

Equity and Access Check

____ I define and clarify for all students what constitutes a "quality question" in the current instructional context, then explain how and why they will use and develop their own questions.

____ I provide models and demonstrate for students a range of such quality questions so they know what these questions look like and can use mine as a guide to craft their own questions.

____ I monitor the progress and understanding of students who struggle to come up with or make effective use of their own questions.

____ I provide a range of interventions, including a scaffolding that begins with complete sets of sample questions students can rely on as they acclimate to using questions in these ways, and then moves to question stems they can complete to develop their own, and finally suggests types of questions they should try to create, or simply topics about which they should develop their own questions.

____ I create opportunities for students to work with their peers as they collaborate to develop or use their quality questions in the current instructional context.

NOTES

MONTH 10

YEAR

LOOKING AHEAD: What is the most important outcome to accomplish by the end of the month—and why?

Notes/Events	Focus 1: What and Why?	Focus 2: What and Why?	Focus 3: What and Why?
	What is your focus and why?	What is your focus and why?	What is your focus and why?

	Focus 1: When and What?	Focus 2: When and What?	Focus 3: When and What?
	When do you work on it and what do you do?	When do you work on it and what do you do?	When do you work on it and what do you do?

The Six Commitments

1. I am committed to the success and well-being of all my students and to their learning.
2. I know my subject and how to teach it so that all my students will learn, remember, and enjoy it.
3. I am responsible for designing, teaching, and assessing the lessons and learning of all my students.
4. I consider equity and access when designing, teaching, and assessing my lessons and students' learning.
5. I reflect on, analyze, and refine my teaching based on feedback from multiple sources.
6. I participate in and contribute to my learning community at school and the profession at large.

Reflect on the one commitment you made the greatest progress on or struggled with the most this month.

HABIT TRACKER DIRECTIONS: List specific **actions** in the left column that will help you develop and maintain healthy habits. Indicate your daily results with a code that works for you. At least some of these habits should be directly related to your three key areas in which you are trying to improve or achieve some specific result this year. Go to jamesclear.com/habit-tracker for more information about tracking your habits.

HABITS	1	2	3	4	5	6	7	8	9	10	11	12	13	14	15	16	17	18	19	20	21	22	23	24	25	26	27	28	29	30	31

LOOKING BACK: What did I do just a little bit better this month? How did I do just a little bit better day by day this month?

PROFESSIONAL: Review and reflect on your weekly self-evaluations for the past month.	**PERSONAL:** Review and reflect on your weekly self-evaluations for the past month.	**KIDS:** Check In/Check On

---

MANAGING YOUR KIDS, CLASSROOM, AND CURRICULUM

FOCUS: COMMUNICATION

*10. Provide **regular communication** about your class, curriculum, or concerns with students, parents, and relevant stakeholders in a timely manner, using whatever means or assistance is appropriate to the situation and student's family.*

What This Means and Why It Matters

Communication with students and their various stakeholders—parents, guardians, counselors, parole officers, to name a few—is a vital part of one's classroom management strategy. Such communication can take the form of periodic emails you send out to all parents as updates on what students have been doing and learning, or information from or links to articles the parents may find helpful (e.g., sleep and the teen brain, stress, online learning during COVID lockdown). It can also be an email to just the parents, for example, about your concerns or praise for their child's recent behavior or academic performance. Whether to include, for example, the student, counselor, or other stakeholders in any of these emails (through a cc or bcc) depends on the urgency, degree of concern, or purpose of the communication. Certain points in the year offer natural and effective opportunities to communicate with parents through a letter sent home: the beginning of the year, end of the grading period or semester, or in the time leading up to final exams. Remember, however, that not all families use or have access to email; sometimes calling is best. In the event that you need a translator, seek help from your administration. If behavior problems persist, meet with the student, parents, and others, such as the counselor or administrator; be sure to follow up with information on the student's response to any agreements from such meetings. It is amazing what a difference a call or email home about a student's recent success (sometimes called "sunshine calls") can make. As many sources note, studies of student achievement in school consistently find parental involvement makes a substantial difference in student learning and behavior and in the perception of the teacher as someone who cares about the student and their success.

Assess yourself by answering T (True), F (False), S (Sometimes)

_____ I communicate with parents and other stakeholders regularly about my class in general and, when appropriate, students' performance, attendance, or behavior specifically.

_____ I communicate with students' counselors or other staff stakeholders any questions or concerns I have about students' academic standing, their performance, or behavior.

_____ I communicate regularly with the teachers, counselors, or other staff about the needs of those students with 504 or IEP plans, or who otherwise warrant attention (those in foster care, identified as Universal Screeners, or any other similar programs).

_____ I monitor, read, and respond to all emails, phone calls, or other communications for updates, reminders, evaluations, or other important information related to students that are time-sensitive or from administration, student health, or mental health departments.

_____ If I receive no response to one mode of communication (email), I follow up with others (phone, regular mail, home visit) and, if necessary, request a translator or student's counselor to help facilitate the discussion.

_____ I look for opportunities to send home positive news and notes that celebrate a student's success or progress in my class.

_____ I consult the student's information files or other relevant documents to gather potentially important and useful background prior to meeting with or having a major meeting about the student.

WORK ON: EXPECTATIONS
THE IMPORTANCE OF HIGH EXPECTATIONS FOR EVERYONE—INCLUDING OURSELVES

Ensuring access to rigorous and intellectually rich learning opportunities is essential for raising multilingual learning achievement. It is essential to disrupt inequitable outcomes with high expectations, strategic scaffolds, and collective efficacy to ensure programs and instruction accelerate, not remediate learning. —Tonya Ward Singer and Diane Staehr Fenner, "From Watering Down to Challenging," *Breaking Down the Wall: Essential Shifts for English Learners' Success*

YEAR

NOTES	Monday	Tuesday	Wednesday

CHECK IN • CHECK UP • CHECK OUT

Visit the TED Talks site (www.ted.com/topics) and find something to watch that will amuse you, inspire you, or teach you something you always wanted to learn. There's something for everyone!

Thursday	Friday	Saturday	Sunday

Brain-Based Learning: Teaching the Way Students Really Learn, 3rd ed. (2020)
Eric Jensen and Liesl McConchie

> "The brain is designed for survival, not
> typical formal instruction" (p. 4).

In the third edition of *Brain-Based Learning*, the authors argue that the brain is designed primarily to focus on what is effective in ensuring its survival and then on what is efficient (p. 2). The authors list three models of learning students typically encounter in the classroom: (1) Survival of the fittest, which they sum up as "You can lead a horse to water, but you can't make it drink"; (2) Determined behaviorist, which they define as "With enough punishment and rewards, you can get any behavior you wish"; and (3) More thoughtful and brain-based, which they summarize as "How can we make the horse thirsty, so that it will want to drink from the trough?" (p. 4). This third model best represents the brain-based approach, which encourages teachers to ask themselves, "How could I discover the learner's natural impediments and built-in motivators so that desired behavior emerges as a natural consequence?" (p. 4). The answer to this question is, in short, that the learning environment must foster the learning you wish to achieve through your instruction.

The authors, using a gardening analogy to explain the learning process, identify five elements for learning to happen and endure: To learn we need the right "context," which they equate with the soil, weather, and other essential conditions; the right "triggers," such as water, to initiate the process; certain "ongoing processes" akin to the seasons and fertilizer, those processes that sustain the process; "systems," such as watering and managing exposure to light; and, finally, "structures" that support and protect the plant, such as stakes, fencing, pruning, or grafting (p. 9). To put it all more plainly, we need to design our assignments and instructional approaches with these "Big Five Players" in mind.

If we do not, students will not learn what we teach (or remember what they learn); nor will what they learn at that point transfer into long-term memory and become part of their subsequent learning.

What to Do

A book such as *Brain-Based Learning* contains a tremendous amount of information and many concepts whose complexity I cannot begin to fit into this brief summary of the book. However, as learning's Big Five Players begin with one of the key principles stressed throughout the planner—the fundamental importance of a safe and engaging learning environment in the classroom—why not begin by having you apply these questions to your own classroom and teaching to examine whether the context of a given lesson, which they describe as the "physical, social, and emotional learning environment" (p. 12) is enhancing or inhibiting students' learning process? Ask yourself these questions:

- Is the learning relevant?
- Is there an urgency to learn it?
- Are my friends here for support?

- How do I feel today? Am I in peak health, or am I a bit under the weather?
- Is the environment well-lit, is fresh air available, and are nearby noises at a minimum?
- Do I have background knowledge on the topic?
- Is there water for hydration?

What to Remember

Besides the Big Five Players outlined above, the most important point to remember when it comes to brain-based learning is summed up in what the authors suggest may be the most important and relevant acronym in their book: R-C-C. R stands for "readiness" to learn or the learner's receptivity. The first C refers to "coherent construction of the learning"; the second C represents consolidation, which involves "error-correction, storage, and transfer" of the content students are learning (p. 165).

Equity and Access Check

____ I clarify what I am teaching and why and link the content of this lesson to prior knowledge and skills my students already learned to ensure that all students are ready to learn the new material.

____ I provide models and demonstrate for students what they will be learning before they learn it to help all students prepare to and be more engaged by the content they will learn.

____ I look for ways to make whatever I am teaching "behaviorally relevant" to all my students to increase their attention and engagement; in other words, I know why I am teaching this lesson but, more importantly, I help all my students understand why they should care about and learn it.

____ I organize the content I am teaching into manageable "chunks" to help all students understand, apply, and remember the content and how it is connected to previous learning.

____ I use a variety of multisensory modes of instruction and such strategies as deliberate practice to help students understand and master more complex or new material they are learning.

NOTES

MONTH 11

YEAR

LOOKING AHEAD: What is the most important outcome to accomplish by the end of the month—and why?

Notes/Events	Focus 1: What and Why?	Focus 2: What and Why?	Focus 3: What and Why?
	What is your focus and why?	What is your focus and why?	What is your focus and why?

	Focus 1: When and What?	Focus 2: When and What?	Focus 3: When and What?
	When do you work on it and what do you do?	When do you work on it and what do you do?	When do you work on it and what do you do?

The Six Commitments

1. I am committed to the success and well-being of all my students and to their learning.
2. I know my subject and how to teach it so that all my students will learn, remember, and enjoy it.
3. I am responsible for designing, teaching, and assessing the lessons and learning of all my students.
4. I consider equity and access when designing, teaching, and assessing my lessons and students' learning.
5. I reflect on, analyze, and refine my teaching based on feedback from multiple sources.
6. I participate in and contribute to my learning community at school and the profession at large.

Reflect on the one commitment you made the greatest progress on or struggled with the most this month.

HABIT TRACKER DIRECTIONS: List specific **actions** in the left column that will help you develop and maintain healthy habits. Indicate your daily results with a code that works for you. At least some of these habits should be directly related to your three key areas in which you are trying to improve or achieve some specific result this year. Go to jamesclear.com/habit-tracker for more information about tracking your habits.

HABITS	1	2	3	4	5	6	7	8	9	10	11	12	13	14	15	16	17	18	19	20	21	22	23	24	25	26	27	28	29	30	31

MONTH 11

LOOKING BACK: What did I do just a little bit better this month? How did I do just a little bit better day by day this month?

PROFESSIONAL: Review and reflect on your weekly self-evaluations for the past month.	PERSONAL: Review and reflect on your weekly self-evaluations for the past month.	KIDS: Check In/Check On

---

MANAGING YOUR KIDS, CLASSROOM, AND CURRICULUM   **FOCUS: MANDATORY POLICIES AND PROCEDURES**

*11. Know and implement all **mandatory policies and procedures** as specified by the state or your district regarding learning accommodations, behavior contracts, or other such agreements.*

What This Means and Why It Matters

We often begin our school year by watching hours of mandatory videos then taking a test to demonstrate our knowledge of how to handle everything from bloodborne pathogens to various types of abuse at school and in our classrooms. These policies and protocols now cover our work in-class, online, and at school-sponsored events. Perhaps most important of all, for most teachers, are the details outlined in 504 or IEPs, because these specify what we must do or provide for students in order to help them learn and succeed. Such accommodations are anchored in the law, which should serve as a reminder and warning about our liability with such students and their families. Increasingly, such interventions are framed using the language of the Multi-Tiered System of Support (MTSS), which the California Department of Education describes as an "integrated, comprehensive framework that focuses on . . . instruction, differentiated learning, student-centered learning, individualized student needs, and the alignment of systems necessary for all students' academic, behavioral, and social success" (2020). In addition to the above-mentioned expectations, we must attend to the other requirements of our job that relate to informing students and parents about events, policies, schedules, assessments, and anything related to emergency drills. Finally, if your school, position, or program requires you to document all interventions or meetings with students in an information management system such as Canvas, be sure to do this with fidelity to protect you in the event of any subsequent legal or administrative challenges.

Assess yourself by answering T (True), F (False), S (Sometimes)

_____ I take accurate attendance each day and submit it as required.

_____ I know and comply with all mandatory reporting protocols as they apply to attendance, discipline, special education, English learners, and any other local, state, or federal program requirements.

_____ I know all emergency procedures, routes, and established locations; they are posted as required for easy reference in case of emergency.

_____ I have all the supplies, including an emergency medical bag with a copy of my current roster, secured and stored near the door for easy access in case of emergency evacuation.

_____ I have immediate access to all 504 and IEP accommodations so I can be sure my lessons comply with all required accommodations.

_____ I do not assign any work that requires materials, technology, or resources, such as books, that are not available to all students. (In some states, such as California, there are laws that prevent teachers from requiring students to purchase books or materials.)

_____ I require all students to learn about and abide by protocols and policies when working online, to ensure that their practices are safe, legal, and ethical in their use of digital tools, intellectual rights, and property; moreover, I ensure that students protect their privacy and personal data.

WORK ON: SOCIAL EMOTIONAL LEARNING
THE ROLE OF EMOTION IN THE PROCESS OF LEARNING

I regularly ask people I work with what the greatest impediment to learning is. It's one of those impossibly large questions, and they normally hesitate a long time to answer. . . . I suspect they are thinking about some aspect of instruction, or access to instruction, poverty, and racism, something like that. But when I suggest that embarrassment is a likely answer, they usually nod their heads. . . . In fact, many of these disadvantages, like racism and poverty, are experienced as ever-present embarrassment or shame—the sense of being an intruder, being unfamiliar with routines that seem second nature to others, fumbling for words and appearing unintelligent. —Tom Newkirk, *Embarrassment and the Emotional Underlife of Learning*

MONTH 11 — YEAR

NOTES	Monday	Tuesday	Wednesday

CHECK IN • CHECK UP • CHECK OUT

Visit The School of Life website (www. theschooloflife.com) to learn more about any topic as you prepare for summer or approach the year's end.

Thursday	Friday	Saturday	Sunday

MONTH 11

WORK ON: PERSEVERENCE
THE ROLE OF GRIT AND PATIENCE IN THE LEARNING PROCESS

Mastery requires patience. The San Antonio Spurs, one of the most successful teams in NBA history, have a quote from social reformer Jacob Riis hanging in their locker room: "When nothing seems to help, I go and look at a stonecutter hammering away at his rock, perhaps a hundred times without as much as a crack showing in it. Yet at the hundred and first blow it will split in two, and I know it was not that last blow that did it—but all that had gone before." —James Clear, *Atomic Habits*

MONTH 12   YEAR

NOTES	Monday	Tuesday	Wednesday

CHECK IN • CHECK UP • CHECK OUT

Visit Cal Newport's website (www.calnewport.com) to learn how to manage your time, better handle email, and do more "deep work." As a bonus, check out his "study hacks" for kids.

MONTH 12

Thursday	Friday	Saturday	Sunday

MONTH 12

Directions: Pause here to review and reflect on how things went for you professionally and personally this year. This page asks you to look back over the past year and evaluate what has and has not worked for you as a teacher, for your PLC as a group, and for you as a person with many obligations outside the classroom, including the obligation to take care of yourself, your family, and your friends.

PROFESSIONAL The Six Commitments	TEAM The Six Characteristics	PERSONAL The Six Categories Of Well-Being
1. **Success and Well-Being**: I am committed to the success and well-being of all my students and to their learning.	1. **Structural Conditions**: How well do our schedules and systems ensure effective collaboration and reduce isolation?	1. **Contentment**: I felt good about things in general this year.
2. **Subject Matter Knowledge**: I know my subject and how to teach it so that all my students will learn, remember, and enjoy it.	2. **Supportive Relational Conditions**: How much do we trust and respect each other, and feel we can speak honestly about our work?	2. **Connection**: I felt connected to my friends, family, community, and interests this year.
3. **Designing, Teaching, Assessing**: I am responsible for designing, teaching, and assessing the lessons and learning of all my students.	3. **Shared Values and Vision**: To what extent do we share the same goal, vision, and beliefs about student learning and our impact on it?	3. **Condition**: I felt physically, mentally, and spiritually/existentially healthy over the course of this past year.
4. **Equity and Access**: I consider equity and access when designing, teaching, and assessing my lessons and students' learning.	4. **Intentional Collective Learning**: How well do we share our knowledge, practices, skills, and strategies about what impacts learning?	4. **Commitments**: I met all of my obligations to myself and others during this school year.
5. **Feedback on Teaching**: I reflect on, analyze, and refine my teaching based on feedback from multiple sources.	5. **Peers Supporting Peers**: To what extent and in what ways do the members of our team celebrate and support each other?	5. **Control**: I felt like I was in control of my life and its demands since school began.
6. **Professional Community**: I participate in and contribute to my learning community at school and the profession at large.	6. **Shared and Supportive Leadership**: How do we share power, authority, and decision making? How is our relationship with the leaders and administrators?	6. **Concerns**: My three greatest concerns this year have been: _____ _____ _____ _____ _____

LOOKING AHEAD: END OF THE YEAR TWO-WAY REFLECTION
PROFESSIONAL AND PERSONAL

Directions: As you think ahead to next year, consider how you would like things to change for you professionally and personally. Keep in mind what has and has not worked for you as a teacher, a team, and a person this year. What small changes can you make to improve things a little bit each day when you come back in the fall?

PROFESSIONAL The Six Commitments	PLC The Six Characteristics	PERSONAL The Six Categories Of Well-Being
1. **Success and Well-Being**: I am committed to the success and well-being of all my students and to their learning. 2. **Subject Matter Knowledge**: I know my subject and how to teach it so that all my students will learn, remember, and enjoy it. 3. **Designing, Teaching, Assessing**: I am responsible for designing, teaching, and assessing the lessons and learning of all my students. 4. **Equity and Access**: I consider equity and access when designing, teaching, and assessing my lessons and students' learning. 5. **Feedback on Teaching**: I reflect on, analyze, and refine my teaching based on feedback from multiple sources. 6. **Professional Community**: I participate in and contribute to my learning community at school and the profession at large.	1. **Structural Conditions**: How well do our schedules and systems ensure effective collaboration and reduce isolation? 2. **Supportive Relational Conditions**: How much do we trust and respect each other, and feel we can speak honestly about our work? 3. **Shared Values and Vision**: To what extent do we share the same goal, vision, and beliefs about student learning and our impact on it? 4. **Intentional Collective Learning**: How well do we share our knowledge, practices, skills, and strategies about what impacts learning? 5. **Peers Supporting Peers**: To what extent and in what ways do the members of our team celebrate and support each other? 6. **Shared and Supportive Leadership**: How do we share power, authority, and decision making? How is our relationship with the leaders and administrators?	1. **Contentment**: I felt good about things in general this year. 2. **Connection**: I felt connected to my friends, family, community, and interests this year. 3. **Condition**: I felt physically, mentally, and spiritually/existentially healthy this year. 4. **Commitments**: I met all of my obligations to myself and others this year. 5. **Control**: I felt like I was in control of my life and its demands this year. 6. **Concerns**: My three greatest concerns this year have been: _____ _____ _____

THE **WEEK** SECTION

It's alarming to face the prospect that you might never truly feel as though you know what you're doing, in work, marriage, parenting, or anything else. But it's liberating, too, because it removes a central reason for feeling self-conscious or inhibited about your performance in those domains in the present moment: if the feeling of total authority is never going to arrive, you might as well not wait any longer to give such activities your all—to put bold plans into practice, to stop erring on the side of caution. It is even more liberating to reflect that everyone else is in the same boat, whether they're aware of it or not.

—Oliver Burkeman, *Four Thousand Weeks: Time Management for Mortals*

MY PERSONAL SIDE

1 **CONTENTMENT:** I felt good about things in general this week.

  never   rarely   sometimes   usually   always

2 **CONNECTION:** I felt connected to my friends, family, community, and interests this week.

  never   rarely   sometimes   usually   always

3 **CONDITION:** I felt physically, mentally, and spiritually/existentially healthy this week.

  never   rarely   sometimes   usually   always

4 **COMMITMENTS:** I met all of my obligations to myself and others this week.

  never   rarely   sometimes   usually   always

5 **CONTROL:** I felt like I was in control of my life and its demands this week.

  never   rarely   sometimes   usually   always

6 **CONCERNS:** This week, my most urgent personal concerns are:

WEEK / · /	Monday	Tuesday
	NOTES	
Students of Concern This Week		
Things to Do This Week		

☐ DO √ DONE ✗ DISMISS ▲ DELEGATE ▶ DEFER

MY PROFESSIONAL SIDE

1 **COMMITMENT:** My commitment and connection to my students and their learning was evident. **never rarely sometimes usually always**

2 **CREDIBILITY:** My teaching reinforced or improved my credibility with my students and colleagues. **never rarely sometimes usually always**

3 **CLARITY:** I made clear each day what students were learning and how they knew they learned it. **never rarely sometimes usually always**

4 **CULTURE:** All of my students felt known, respected, safe, and engaged while in my classroom. **never rarely sometimes usually always**

5 **CONTRIBUTIONS:** I made substantive contributions to my school, department, team, or profession. **never rarely sometimes usually always**

6 **CONCERNS:** This week, my most urgent professional concerns are:

THE EISENHOWER MATRIX

	URGENT	NOT URGENT
IMPORTANT	**DO** Do it now	**DECIDE** Specifically when to do it
UNIMPORTANT	**DELEGATE** Ask someone else	**DELETE** Do not do it

Visit eisenhower.me/eisenhower-matrix/ for more information

Wednesday	Thursday	Friday
NOTES		

WEEK 1

113

JUST CHECKING! THE SIX DIMENSIONS OF WELLNESS

Complete this brief inventory to evaluate your well-being; then, follow the directions on the page to the right.

1 _____ **OCCUPATIONAL:** Despite the inevitable challenges, I am finding my work rewarding and energizing because it offers me a chance to use and develop my knowledge and talents to help students and my colleagues.

2 _____ **PHYSICAL:** Though I had many obligations and demands on my time and energy, I made an effort to maintain a healthy diet, get enough sleep, and exercise to feel well.

3 _____ **SOCIAL:** I had a lot going on this week, but I made time to connect with colleagues and kids, friends and family so that I could contribute to my community and enjoy the relationships I have with people important to me.

4 _____ **INTELLECTUAL:** Yes, I had many responsibilities this week, but I made a point of learning new things that allowed me to deepen my knowledge and improve my skills so I that could identify and solve challenging problems.

5 _____ **SPIRITUAL:** Throughout the week, I have often felt overwhelmed; however, I carved out time to feel and express my gratitude, as well as to think about and act in accordance with my values and beliefs.

6 _____ **EMOTIONAL:** As I navigated the many obstacles I encountered this week, I listened to what I and others felt, guided by the desire to better understand and accept myself and others despite our human limitations.

WEEK / • /		Monday	Tuesday
		NOTES	
Students of Concern This Week			
Things to Do This Week			

☐ DO √ DONE ✕ DISMISS ▲ DELEGATE ▶ DEFER

114

TAKE A MINUTE

Jot down some insights and ideas about what you can do in response to your scores on the previous page. To learn more about the Six Dimensions of Wellness and find some useful tools and strategies, visit nationalwellness.org/tools.

THE HALT CHECKLIST

Hungry	Angry
Why are you hungry?	Why are you angry?
Are you bored?	Is it stress? Anxiety?
Are you dehydrated?	Who/what would help?

Lonely	Tired
Why are you feeling this?	How much are you sleeping?
Online too much/too long?	Are you physically or emotionally tired?
Who can you connect with?	What is your sleep routine?

Visit www.mindtools.com/pages/article/HALT-risk-states.html

Wednesday	Thursday	Friday
NOTES		

CHECK UP AND CHECK IN

Take time to evaluate your mental and emotional health this week; then use the space to the right to reflect on your self-evaluation and the reasons you are feeling as you do this week.

IN CRISIS	STRUGGLING	SURVIVING	THRIVING	EXCELLING
Very anxious	Anxious	Worried	Positive	Cheerful
Very low mood	Depressed	Nervous	Calm	Joyful
Absenteeism	Tired	Irritable	Performing	Energetic
Exhausted	Poor performance	Sad	Sleeping well	High performance
Very poor sleep	Poor sleep	Trouble sleeping	Eating normally	Flow
Weight loss	Poor appetite	Distracted	Normal social activity	Fully realizing potential
		Withdrawn		

WEEK

/ • /

Students of Concern This Week

Things to Do This Week

Monday	Tuesday
NOTES	

☐ DO √ DONE ✗ DISMISS ▲ DELEGATE ▶ DEFER

116

THE EMPATHY MAP

SAYS	THINKS
What someone says about a situation, a person, an experience.	What someone thinks about something (but may not actually say).

WHAT THE PERSON

DOES	FEELS
How someone acts in response to people, a place, a situation, or experience.	What someone feels in response to a person, event, experience, or place.

Visit www.nngroup.com/artides/empathy-mapping/

Wednesday	Thursday	Friday
NOTES		

MY PERSONAL SIDE

1 **CONTENTMENT:** I felt good about things in general this week.

                never   rarely   sometimes   usually   always

2 **CONNECTION:** I felt connected to my friends, family, community, and interests this week.

                never   rarely   sometimes   usually   always

3 **CONDITION:** I felt physically, mentally, and spiritually/existentially healthy this week.

                never   rarely   sometimes   usually   always

4 **COMMITMENTS:** I met all of my obligations to myself and others this week.

                never   rarely   sometimes   usually   always

5 **CONTROL:** I felt like I was in control of my life and its demands this week.

                never   rarely   sometimes   usually   always

6 **CONCERNS:** This week, my most urgent personal concerns are:

WEEK	Monday	Tuesday
/ • /	NOTES	
Students of Concern This Week		
Things to Do This Week		

☐ DO   √ DONE   ✗ DISMISS   ▲ DELEGATE   ▶ DEFER

MY PROFESSIONAL SIDE

1 **COMMITMENT:** My commitment and connection to my students and their learning was evident.   **never**   **rarely**   **sometimes**   **usually**   **always**

2 **CREDIBILITY:** My teaching reinforced or improved my credibility with my students and colleagues.   **never**   **rarely**   **sometimes**   **usually**   **always**

3 **CLARITY:** I made clear each day what students were learning and how they knew they learned it.   **never**   **rarely**   **sometimes**   **usually**   **always**

4 **CULTURE:** All of my students felt known, respected, safe, and engaged while in my classroom.   **never**   **rarely**   **sometimes**   **usually**   **always**

5 **CONTRIBUTIONS:** I made substantive contributions to my school, department, team, or profession.   **never**   **rarely**   **sometimes**   **usually**   **always**

6 **CONCERNS:** This week, my most urgent professional concerns are:

RESPECT	**TRUST**
Does each person feel a sense of agency and feel valued by others?	Is it safe to take risks, to assume others' positive intentions and mutual investment?
OPTIMISM	**INTENTIONALITY**
Does everyone believe others have untapped potential and can learn and succeed with proper support?	Do all people, places, policies, programs, and processes foster feelings of trust, respect, and optimism?

Purkey, William. "Creating Safe Schools Through Invitational Education."

Wednesday	Thursday	Friday

WEEK 4

JUST CHECKING! THE SIX DIMENSIONS OF WELLNESS

1 **CONTENTMENT:** I felt good about things in general this week.

        never   rarely   sometimes   usually   always

2 **CONNECTION:** I felt connected to my friends, family, community, and interests this week.

        never   rarely   sometimes   usually   always

3 **CONDITION:** I felt physically, mentally, and spiritually/existentially healthy this week.

        never   rarely   sometimes   usually   always

4 **COMMITMENTS:** I met all of my obligations to myself and others this week.

        never   rarely   sometimes   usually   always

5 **CONTROL:** I felt like I was in control of my life and its demands this week.

        never   rarely   sometimes   usually   always

6 **CONCERNS:** This week, my most urgent personal concerns are:

WEEK

/ • /

Students of Concern This Week

Things to Do This Week

	Monday	Tuesday
NOTES		

☐ DO √ DONE ✗ DISMISS ▲ DELEGATE ▶ DEFER

TAKE A MINUTE

1 **COMMITMENT:** My commitment and connection to my students and their learning was evident.   never   rarely   sometimes   usually   always

2 **CREDIBILITY:** My teaching reinforced or improved my credibility with my students and colleagues.   never   rarely   sometimes   usually   always

3 **CLARITY:** I made clear each day what students were learning and how they knew they learned it.   never   rarely   sometimes   usually   always

4 **CULTURE:** All of my students felt known, respected, safe, and engaged while in my classroom.   never   rarely   sometimes   usually   always

5 **CONTRIBUTIONS:** I made substantive contributions to my school, department, team, or profession.   never   rarely   sometimes   usually   always

6 **CONCERNS:** This week, my most urgent professional concerns are:

THE PDSA CYCLE

PLAN	DO
Create a plan, method, or process to test a possible strategy for improving teaching/learning.	Test your plan, method, or process; collect data to refine or improve the plan/method.
ACT	**STUDY**
Based on the data, implement, improve, or replace strategy or approach with new one.	Analyse results to identify key insights about what to refine or change to improve the strategy or approach.

Visit deming.org/explore/pdsa/ for more information on the PDSA Cycle

Wednesday	Thursday	Friday
NOTES		

CHECK UP AND CHECK IN

Take time to evaluate your mental and emotional health this week; then use the space to the right to reflect on your self-evaluation and the reasons you are feeling as you do this week.

IN CRISIS	STRUGGLING	SURVIVING	THRIVING	EXCELLING
Very anxious	Anxious	Worried	Positive	Cheerful
Very low mood	Depressed	Nervous	Calm	Joyful
Absenteeism	Tired	Irritable	Performing	Energetic
Exhausted	Poor performance	Sad	Sleeping well	High performance
Very poor sleep	Poor sleep	Trouble sleeping	Eating normally	Flow
Weight loss	Poor appetite	Distracted	Normal social activity	Fully realizing potential
		Withdrawn		

WEEK

/ • /

Students of Concern This Week

Things to Do This Week

☐ DO ✓ DONE ✗ DISMISS ▲ DELEGATE ▶ DEFER

	Monday	Tuesday
NOTES		

_____

_____

_____

_____

_____

_____

_____

_____

_____

_____

_____

_____

INCORPORATE MULTIPLE LITERACIES

ACADEMIC	CULTURAL
What skills and strategies can students use to handle these cognitively demanding tasks?	What knowledge of past/present events do students need to consider? Are there connections to one's culture?
SOCIAL	EMOTIONAL
How can I help students navigate different settings, viewpoints, and needs when communicating ideas?	What emotions does this arouse and how can one learn to manage such feelings and beliefs?

Teaching Reading to Black Adolescent Males: Closing the Achievement Gap,
Alfred Tatum (2005, 35)

Wednesday	Thursday	Friday
NOTES		

WEEK 6

NOTES

Use this page to jot down notes from the past six weeks to help you understand what you got right, what you still wonder, and what you need to keep working on or learning more about.

NOTES

Use this page to jot down notes based on the past six weeks to help you understand what you can do to improve in the key areas you have identified as important this year.

MY PERSONAL SIDE

1 **CONTENTMENT:** I felt good about things in general this week.

            never   rarely   sometimes   usually   always

2 **CONNECTION:** I felt connected to my friends, family, community, and interests this week.

            never   rarely   sometimes   usually   always

3 **CONDITION:** I felt physically, mentally, and spiritually/existentially healthy this week.

            never   rarely   sometimes   usually   always

4 **COMMITMENTS:** I met all of my obligations to myself and others this week.

            never   rarely   sometimes   usually   always

5 **CONTROL:** I felt like I was in control of my life and its demands this week.

            never   rarely   sometimes   usually   always

6 **CONCERNS:** This week, my most urgent personal concerns are:

WEEK /   /   •   /

Students of Concern This Week

Things to Do This Week

	Monday	Tuesday
NOTES		

□ DO   √ DONE   ✕ DISMISS   ▲ DELEGATE   ▶ DEFER

MY PROFESSIONAL SIDE

1 **COMMITMENT:** My commitment and connection to my students and their learning was
   evident.   **never**   **rarely**   **sometimes**   **usually**   **always**

2 **CREDIBILITY:** My teaching reinforced or improved my credibility with my students and
   colleagues.   **never**   **rarely**   **sometimes**   **usually**   **always**

3 **CLARITY:** I made clear each day what students were learning and how they knew they
   learned it.   **never**   **rarely**   **sometimes**   **usually**   **always**

4 **CULTURE:** All of my students felt known, respected, safe, and engaged while in my
   classroom.   **never**   **rarely**   **sometimes**   **usually**   **always**

5 **CONTRIBUTIONS:** I made substantive contributions to my school, department, team, or
   profession.   **never**   **rarely**   **sometimes**   **usually**   **always**

6 **CONCERNS:** This week, my most urgent professional concerns are:

Visit eisenhower.me/eisenhower-matrix/
for more information

THE EISENHOWER MATRIX

	URGENT	NOT URGENT
IMPORTANT	**DO** Do it now	**DECIDE** Specifically when to do it
UNIMPORTANT	**DELEGATE** Ask someone else	**DELETE** Do not do it

Wednesday	Thursday	Friday
Notes		

JUST CHECKING! THE SIX DIMENSIONS OF WELLNESS

Complete this brief inventory to evaluate your wellbeing; then follow the directions on the page to the right.

1 _____ **OCCUPATIONAL:** Despite the inevitable challenges, I am finding my work rewarding and energizing because it offers me a chance to use and develop my knowledge and talents to help my students and colleagues.

2 _____ **PHYSICAL:** Though I had many obligations and demands on my time and energy, I made an effort to maintain a healthy diet, get enough sleep, and exercise to feel well.

3 _____ **SOCIAL:** I had a lot going on this week, but I made time to connect with colleagues and kids, friends and family so that I could contribute to my community and enjoy the relationships I have with people important to me.

4 _____ **INTELLECTUAL:** Yes, I had many responsibilities this week, but I made a point of learning new things that allowed me to deepen my knowledge and improve my skills so that I could identify and solve challenging problems.

5 _____ **SPIRITUAL:** Throughout the week, I have often felt overwhelmed; however, I carved out time to feel and express my gratitude, as well as to think about and act in accordance with my values and beliefs.

6 _____ **EMOTIONAL:** As I navigated the many obstacles I encountered this week, I listened to what I and others felt, guided by the desire to better understand and accept myself and others despite our human limitations.

WEEK / • /	Monday	Tuesday
	NOTES	
Students of Concern This Week		
Things to Do This Week		

☐ DO √ DONE ✕ DISMISS ▲ DELEGATE ▶ DEFER

TAKE A MINUTE

Jot down some insights and ideas about what you can do in response to your scores on the previous page. To learn more about the Six Dimensions of Wellness and find some useful tools and strategies, visit nationalwellness.org/tools.

Visit www.mindtools.com/pages/article/HALT-risk-states.html

THE HALT CHECKLIST

Hungry	Angry
Why are you hungry?	Why are you angry?
Are you bored?	Is it stress? Anxiety?
Are you dehydrated?	Who/what would help?

Lonely	Tired
Why are you feeling this?	How much are you sleeping?
Online too much/too long?	Are you physically or emotionally tired?
Who can you connect with?	What is your sleep routine?

Wednesday	Thursday	Friday
NOTES		

CHECK UP AND CHECK IN

Take time to evaluate your mental and emotional health this week; then use the space to the right to reflect on your self-evaluation and the reasons you are feeling as you do this week.

IN CRISIS	STRUGGLING	SURVIVING	THRIVING	EXCELLING
Very anxious	Anxious	Worried	Positive	Cheerful
Very low mood	Depressed	Nervous	Calm	Joyful
Absenteeism	Tired	Irritable	Performing	Energetic
Exhausted	Poor performance	Sad	Sleeping well	High performance
Very poor sleep	Poor sleep	Trouble sleeping	Eating normally	Flow
Weight loss	Poor appetite	Distracted	Normal social activity	Fully realizing potential
		Withdrawn		

WEEK

/ • /

Students of Concern This Week

Things to Do This Week

	Monday	Tuesday
NOTES		

☐ DO √ DONE ✕ DISMISS ▲ DELEGATE ▶ DEFER

THE EMPATHY MAP

SAYS	**THINKS**
What someone says about a situation, a person, an experience.	What someone thinks about something (but may not actually say).

WHAT THE PERSON

DOES	**FEELS**
How someone acts in response to people, a place, a situation, or experience.	What someone feels in response to a person, event, experience, or place.

Visit www.nngroup.com/artides/empathy-mapping/

Wednesday	Thursday	Friday
Notes		

MY PERSONAL SIDE

1 **CONTENTMENT:** I felt good about things in general this week.

        never   rarely   sometimes   usually   always

2 **CONNECTION:** I felt connected to my friends, family, community, and interests this week.

        never   rarely   sometimes   usually   always

3 **CONDITION:** I felt physically, mentally, and spiritually/existentially healthy this week.

        never   rarely   sometimes   usually   always

4 **COMMITMENTS:** I met all of my obligations to myself and others this week.

        never   rarely   sometimes   usually   always

5 **CONTROL:** I felt like I was in control of my life and its demands this week.

        never   rarely   sometimes   usually   always

6 **CONCERNS:** This week, my most urgent personal concerns are:

WEEK / • /	Monday	Tuesday
NOTES		
Students of Concern This Week		
Things to Do This Week		

☐ DO   √ DONE   ✕ DISMISS   ▲ DELEGATE   ▶ DEFER

MY PROFESSIONAL SIDE

1 **COMMITMENT:** My commitment and connection to my students and their learning was evident. **never** **rarely** **sometimes** **usually** **always**

2 **CREDIBILITY:** My teaching reinforced or improved my credibility with my students and colleagues. **never** **rarely** **sometimes** **usually** **always**

3 **CLARITY:** I made clear each day what students were learning and how they knew they learned it. **never** **rarely** **sometimes** **usually** **always**

4 **CULTURE:** All of my students felt known, respected, safe, and engaged while in my classroom. **never** **rarely** **sometimes** **usually** **always**

5 **CONTRIBUTIONS:** I made substantive contributions to my school, department, team, or profession. **never** **rarely** **sometimes** **usually** **always**

6 **CONCERNS:** This week, my most urgent professional concerns are:

RESPECT	TRUST
Does each person feel a sense of agency and feel valued by others?	Is it safe to take risks, to assume others' positive intentions and mutual investment?
OPTIMISM	**INTENTIONALITY**
Does everyone believe others have untapped potential and can learn and succeed with proper support?	Do all people, places, policies, programs, and processes foster feelings of trust, respect, and optimism?

Purkey, William. "Creating Safe Schools Through Invitational Education."

Wednesday	Thursday	Friday
NOTES		

JUST CHECKING! THE SIX DIMENSIONS OF WELLNESS

1 **CONTENTMENT:** I felt good about things in general this week.

               never   rarely   sometimes   usually   always

2 **CONNECTION:** I felt connected to my friends, family, community, and interests this week.

               never   rarely   sometimes   usually   always

3 **CONDITION:** I felt physically, mentally, and spiritually/existentially healthy this week.

               never   rarely   sometimes   usually   always

4 **COMMITMENTS:** I met all of my obligations to myself and others this week.

               never   rarely   sometimes   usually   always

5 **CONTROL:** I felt like I was in control of my life and its demands this week.

               never   rarely   sometimes   usually   always

6 **CONCERNS:** This week, my most urgent personal concerns are:

WEEK	Monday	Tuesday
/ • /	NOTES	
Students of Concern This Week		

Things to Do This Week

□ DO √ DONE ✕ DISMISS ▲ DELEGATE ▶ DEFER

1 **COMMITMENT:** My commitment and connection to my students and their learning was evident.   **never**   **rarely**   **sometimes**   **usually**   **always**

2 **CREDIBILITY:** My teaching reinforced or improved my credibility with my students and colleagues.   **never**   **rarely**   **sometimes**   **usually**   **always**

3 **CLARITY:** I made clear each day what students were learning and how they knew they learned it.   **never**   **rarely**   **sometimes**   **usually**   **always**

4 **CULTURE:** All of my students felt known, respected, safe, and engaged while in my classroom.   **never**   **rarely**   **sometimes**   **usually**   **always**

5 **CONTRIBUTIONS:** I made substantive contributions to my school, department, team, or profession.   **never**   **rarely**   **sometimes**   **usually**   **always**

6 **CONCERNS:** This week, my most urgent professional concerns are:

THE PDSA CYCLE

PLAN	DO
Create a plan, method, or process to test a possible strategy for improving teaching/ learning.	Test your plan, method, or process; collect data to refine or improve the plan/method.
ACT	**STUDY**
Based on the data, implement, improve, or replace strategy or approach with new one.	Analyse results to identify key insights about what to refine or change to improve the strategy or approach.

Visit deming.org/explore/pdsa/ for more information on the PDSA Cycle

Wednesday	Thursday	Friday
NOTE:		

CHECK UP AND CHECK IN

Take time to evaluate your mental and emotional health this week; then use the space to the right to reflect on your self-evaluation and the reasons you are feeling as you do this week.

IN CRISIS	STRUGGLING	SURVIVING	THRIVING	EXCELLING
Very anxious	Anxious	Worried	Positive	Cheerful
Very low mood	Depressed	Nervous	Calm	Joyful
Absenteeism	Tired	Irritable	Performing	Energetic
Exhausted	Poor performance	Sad	Sleeping well	High performance
Very poor sleep	Poor sleep	Trouble sleeping	Eating normally	Flow
Weight loss	Poor appetite	Distracted	Normal social activity	Fully realizing potential
		Withdrawn		

WEEK

/ • /

	Monday	Tuesday
	NOTES	

Students of Concern This Week

Things to Do This Week

☐ DO ✓ DONE ✗ DISMISS ▲ DELEGATE ▶ DEFER

136

_____
_____
_____
_____
_____
_____

_____
_____
_____
_____
_____

ACADEMIC	CULTURAL
What skills and strategies can students use to handle these cognitively demanding tasks?	What knowledge of past/present events do students need to consider? Are there connections to one's culture?
SOCIAL	**EMOTIONAL**
How can I help students navigate different settings, viewpoints, and needs when communicating ideas?	What emotions does this arouse and how can one learn to manage such feelings and beliefs?

Teaching Reading to Black Adolescent Males: Closing the Achievement Gap,
Alfred Tatum (2005, 35)

Wednesday	Thursday	Friday
Notes		

NOTES

Use this page to jot down notes from the past six weeks to help you understand what you got right, what you still wonder, and what you need to keep working on or learning more about.

NOTES

Use this page to jot down notes based on the past six weeks to help you understand what you can do to improve in the key areas you have identified as important this year.

MY PERSONAL SIDE

1 **CONTENTMENT:** I felt good about things in general this week.

           never   rarely   sometimes   usually   always

2 **CONNECTION:** I felt connected to my friends, family, community, and interests this week.

           never   rarely   sometimes   usually   always

3 **CONDITION:** I felt physically, mentally, and spiritually/existentially healthy this week.

           never   rarely   sometimes   usually   always

4 **COMMITMENTS:** I met all of my obligations to myself and others this week.

           never   rarely   sometimes   usually   always

5 **CONTROL:** I felt like I was in control of my life and its demands this week.

           never   rarely   sometimes   usually   always

6 **CONCERNS:** This week, my most urgent personal concerns are:

WEEK / • /	Monday	Tuesday
	NOTES	
Students of Concern This Week		
Things to Do This Week		

☐ DO   √ DONE   ✗ DISMISS   ▲ DELEGATE   ▶ DEFER

MY PROFESSIONAL SIDE

1 **COMMITMENT:** My commitment and connection to my students and their learning was evident.   **never**   **rarely**   **sometimes**   **usually**   **always**

2 **CREDIBILITY:** My teaching reinforced or improved my credibility with my students and colleagues.   **never**   **rarely**   **sometimes**   **usually**   **always**

3 **CLARITY:** I made clear each day what students were learning and how they knew they learned it.   **never**   **rarely**   **sometimes**   **usually**   **always**

4 **CULTURE:** All of my students felt known, respected, safe, and engaged while in my classroom.   **never**   **rarely**   **sometimes**   **usually**   **always**

5 **CONTRIBUTIONS:** I made substantive contributions to my school, department, team, or profession.   **never**   **rarely**   **sometimes**   **usually**   **always**

6 **CONCERNS:** This week, my most urgent professional concerns are:

THE EISENHOWER MATRIX

	URGENT	NOT URGENT
IMPORTANT	**DO** Do it now	**DECIDE** Specifically when to do it
UNIMPORTANT	**DELEGATE** Ask someone else	**DELETE** Do not do it

Visit eisenhower.me/eisenhower-matrix/ for more information

Wednesday	Thursday	Friday
NOTES		

JUST CHECKING! THE SIX DIMENSIONS OF WELLNESS

Complete this brief inventory to evaluate your wellbeing; then follow the directions on the page to the right.

1 _____ **OCCUPATIONAL:** Despite the inevitable challenges, I am finding my work rewarding and energizing because it offers me a chance to use and develop my knowledge and talents to help my students and colleagues.

2 _____ **PHYSICAL:** Though I had many obligations and demands on my time and energy, I made an effort to maintain a healthy diet, get enough sleep, and exercise to feel well.

3 _____ **SOCIAL:** I had a lot going on this week, but I made time to connect with colleagues and kids, friends and family so that I could contribute to my community and enjoy the relationships I have with people important to me.

4 _____ **INTELLECTUAL:** Yes, I had many responsibilities this week, but I made a point of learning new things that allowed me to deepen my knowledge and improve my skills so that I could identify and solve challenging problems.

5 _____ **SPIRITUAL:** Throughout the week, I have often felt overwhelmed; however, I carved out time to feel and express my gratitude, as well as to think about and act in accordance with my values and beliefs.

6 _____ **EMOTIONAL:** As I navigated the many obstacles I encountered this week, I listened to what I and others felt, guided by the desire to better understand and accept myself and others despite our human limitations.

WEEK / • /	Monday	Tuesday
Students of Concern This Week	NOTES	

Things to Do This Week

☐ DO √ DONE ✕ DISMISS ▲ DELEGATE ▶ DEFER

TAKE A MINUTE

Jot down some insights and ideas about what you can do in response to your scores on the previous page. To learn more about the Six Dimensions of Wellness and find some useful tools and strategies, visit nationalwellness.org/tools.

_____

_____

_____

_____

_____

Wednesday	Thursday	Friday
NOTES		

CHECK UP AND CHECK IN

Take time to evaluate your mental and emotional health this week; then use the space to the right to reflect on your self-evaluation and the reasons you are feeling as you do this week.

IN CRISIS	STRUGGLING	SURVIVING	THRIVING	EXCELLING
Very anxious	Anxious	Worried	Positive	Cheerful
Very low mood	Depressed	Nervous	Calm	Joyful
Absenteeism	Tired	Irritable	Performing	Energetic
Exhausted	Poor performance	Sad	Sleeping well	High performance
Very poor sleep	Poor sleep	Trouble sleeping	Eating normally	Flow
Weight loss	Poor appetite	Distracted	Normal social activity	Fully realizing potential
		Withdrawn		

WEEK

/ • /

Students of Concern This Week

Things to Do This Week

	Monday	Tuesday
NOTES		

□ DO √ DONE ✗ DISMISS ▲ DELEGATE ▶ DEFER

THE EMPATHY MAP

SAYS	THINKS
What someone says about a situation, a person, an experience.	What someone thinks about something (but may not actually say).

WHAT THE PERSON

DOES	FEELS
How someone acts in response to people, a place, a situation, or experience.	What someone feels in response to a person, event, experience, or place.

Visit www.nngroup.com/artides/empathy-mapping/

Wednesday	Thursday	Friday
NOTES		

MY PERSONAL SIDE

1 **CONTENTMENT:** I felt good about things in general this week.

        never   rarely   sometimes   usually   always

2 **CONNECTION:** I felt connected to my friends, family, community, and interests this week.

        never   rarely   sometimes   usually   always

3 **CONDITION:** I felt physically, mentally, and spiritually/existentially healthy this week.

        never   rarely   sometimes   usually   always

4 **COMMITMENTS:** I met all of my obligations to myself and others this week.

        never   rarely   sometimes   usually   always

5 **CONTROL:** I felt like I was in control of my life and its demands this week.

        never   rarely   sometimes   usually   always

6 **CONCERNS:** This week, my most urgent personal concerns are:

WEEK

/   •   /

	Monday	Tuesday
Students of Concern This Week	NOTES	

Things to Do This Week

☐ DO   √ DONE   ✕ DISMISS   ▲ DELEGATE   ▶ DEFER

MY PROFESSIONAL SIDE

1 **COMMITMENT:** My commitment and connection to my students and their learning was evident.   **never   rarely   sometimes   usually   always**

2 **CREDIBILITY:** My teaching reinforced or improved my credibility with my students and colleagues.   **never   rarely   sometimes   usually   always**

3 **CLARITY:** I made clear each day what students were learning and how they knew they learned it.   **never   rarely   sometimes   usually   always**

4 **CULTURE:** All of my students felt known, respected, safe, and engaged while in my classroom.   **never   rarely   sometimes   usually   always**

5 **CONTRIBUTIONS:** I made substantive contributions to my school, department, team, or profession.   **never   rarely   sometimes   usually   always**

6 **CONCERNS:** This week, my most urgent professional concerns are:

RESPECT Does each person feel a sense of agency and feel valued by others?	**TRUST** Is it safe to take risks, to assume others' positive intentions and mutual investment?
OPTIMISM Does everyone believe others have untapped potential and can learn and succeed with proper support?	**INTENTIONALITY** Do all people, places, policies, programs, and processes foster feelings of trust, respect, and optimism?

Purkey, William. "Creating Safe Schools Through Invitational Education."

Wednesday	Thursday	Friday
NOTES		

JUST CHECKING! THE SIX DIMENSIONS OF WELLNESS

1 **CONTENTMENT:** I felt good about things in general this week.

  never   rarely   sometimes   usually   always

2 **CONNECTION:** I felt connected to my friends, family, community, and interests this week.

  never   rarely   sometimes   usually   always

3 **CONDITION:** I felt physically, mentally, and spiritually/existentially healthy this week.

  never   rarely   sometimes   usually   always

4 **COMMITMENTS:** I met all of my obligations to myself and others this week.

  never   rarely   sometimes   usually   always

5 **CONTROL:** I felt like I was in control of my life and its demands this week.

  never   rarely   sometimes   usually   always

6 **CONCERNS:** This week, my most urgent personal concerns are:

		Monday	Tuesday
WEEK		NOTES	
/ • /			
Students of Concern This Week			

Things to Do This Week

☐ DO √ DONE ✗ DISMISS ▲ DELEGATE ▶ DEFER

148

TAKE A MINUTE

1 **COMMITMENT:** My commitment and connection to my students and their learning was evident.   **never**   **rarely**   **sometimes**   **usually**   **always**

2 **CREDIBILITY:** My teaching reinforced or improved my credibility with my students and colleagues.   **never**   **rarely**   **sometimes**   **usually**   **always**

3 **CLARITY:** I made clear each day what students were learning and how they knew they learned it.   **never**   **rarely**   **sometimes**   **usually**   **always**

4 **CULTURE:** All of my students felt known, respected, safe, and engaged while in my classroom.   **never**   **rarely**   **sometimes**   **usually**   **always**

5 **CONTRIBUTIONS:** I made substantive contributions to my school, department, team, or profession.   **never**   **rarely**   **sometimes**   **usually**   **always**

6 **CONCERNS:** This week, my most urgent professional concerns are:

THE PDSA CYCLE

PLAN	DO
Create a plan, method, or process to test a possible strategy for improving teaching/ learning.	Test your plan, method, or process; collect data to refine or improve the plan/method.
ACT	**STUDY**
Based on the data, implement, improve, or replace strategy or approach with new one.	Analyse results to identify key insights about what to refine or change to improve the strategy or approach.

Visit deming.org/explore/pdsa/ for more information on the PDSA Cycle

Wednesday	Thursday	Friday
NOTES		

WEEK 17

149

CHECK UP AND CHECK IN

Take time to evaluate your mental and emotional health this week; then use the space to the right to reflect on your self-evaluation and the reasons you are feeling as you do this week.

IN CRISIS	STRUGGLING	SURVIVING	THRIVING	EXCELLING
Very anxious	Anxious	Worried	Positive	Cheerful
Very low mood	Depressed	Nervous	Calm	Joyful
Absenteeism	Tired	Irritable	Performing	Energetic
Exhausted	Poor performance	Sad	Sleeping well	High performance
Very poor sleep	Poor sleep	Trouble sleeping	Eating normally	Flow
Weight loss	Poor appetite	Distracted	Normal social activity	Fully realizing potential
		Withdrawn		

WEEK

/ • /

Students of Concern This Week

Things to Do This Week

	Monday	Tuesday
NOTES		

□ DO ✓ DONE ✗ DISMISS ▲ DELEGATE ▶ DEFER

INCORPORATE MULTIPLE LITERACIES

ACADEMIC	CULTURAL
What skills and strategies can students use to handle these cognitively demanding tasks?	What knowledge of past/present events do students need to consider? Are there connections to one's culture?
SOCIAL	EMOTIONAL
How can I help students navigate different settings, viewpoints, and needs when communicating ideas?	What emotions does this arouse and how can one learn to manage such feelings and beliefs?

Teaching Reading to Black Adolescent Males: Closing the Achievement Gap,
Alfred Tatum (2005, 35)

Wednesday	Thursday	Friday
NOTES		

NOTES

Use this page to jot down notes from the past six weeks to help you understand what you got right, what you still wonder, and what you need to keep working on or learning more about.

NOTES

Use this page to jot down notes based on the past six weeks to help you understand what you can do to improve in the key areas you have identified as important this year.

MY PERSONAL SIDE

1 **CONTENTMENT:** I felt good about things in general this week.

     never   rarely   sometimes   usually   always

2 **CONNECTION:** I felt connected to my friends, family, community, and interests this week.

     never   rarely   sometimes   usually   always

3 **CONDITION:** I felt physically, mentally, and spiritually/existentially healthy this week.

     never   rarely   sometimes   usually   always

4 **COMMITMENTS:** I met all of my obligations to myself and others this week.

     never   rarely   sometimes   usually   always

5 **CONTROL:** I felt like I was in control of my life and its demands this week.

     never   rarely   sometimes   usually   always

6 **CONCERNS:** This week, my most urgent personal concerns are:

WEEK	Monday	Tuesday
/ • /	NOTES	
Students of Concern This Week		
Things to Do This Week		

☐ DO   √ DONE   ✗ DISMISS   ▲ DELEGATE   ▶ DEFER

MY PROFESSIONAL SIDE

1 **COMMITMENT:** My commitment and connection to my students and their learning was evident.   **never**   **rarely**   **sometimes**   **usually**   **always**

2 **CREDIBILITY:** My teaching reinforced or improved my credibility with my students and colleagues.   **never**   **rarely**   **sometimes**   **usually**   **always**

3 **CLARITY:** I made clear each day what students were learning and how they knew they learned it.   **never**   **rarely**   **sometimes**   **usually**   **always**

4 **CULTURE:** All of my students felt known, respected, safe, and engaged while in my classroom.   **never**   **rarely**   **sometimes**   **usually**   **always**

5 **CONTRIBUTIONS:** I made substantive contributions to my school, department, team, or profession.   **never**   **rarely**   **sometimes**   **usually**   **always**

6 **CONCERNS:** This week, my most urgent professional concerns are:

THE EISENHOWER MATRIX

	URGENT	NOT URGENT
IMPORTANT	**DO** Do it now	**DECIDE** Specifically when to do it
UNIMPORTANT	**DELEGATE** Ask someone else	**DELETE** Do not do it

Visit eisenhower.me/eisenhower-matrix/ for more information

Wednesday	Thursday	Friday
NOTES		

JUST CHECKING! THE SIX DIMENSIONS OF WELLNESS

Complete this brief inventory to evaluate your wellbeing; then follow the directions on the page to the right.

1 _____ **OCCUPATIONAL:** Despite the inevitable challenges, I am finding my work rewarding and energizing because it offers me a chance to use and develop my knowledge and talents to help my students and colleagues.

2 _____ **PHYSICAL:** Though I had many obligations and demands on my time and energy, I made an effort to maintain a healthy diet, get enough sleep, and exercise to feel well.

3 _____ **SOCIAL:** I had a lot going on this week, but I made time to connect with colleagues and kids, friends and family so that I could contribute to my community and enjoy the relationships I have with people important to me.

4 _____ **INTELLECTUAL:** Yes, I had many responsibilities this week, but I made a point of learning new things that allowed me to deepen my knowledge and improve my skills so that I could identify and solve challenging problems.

5 _____ **SPIRITUAL:** Throughout the week, I have often felt overwhelmed; however, I carved out time to feel and express my gratitude, as well as to think about and act in accordance with my values and beliefs.

6 _____ **EMOTIONAL:** As I navigated the many obstacles I encountered this week, I listened to what I and others felt, guided by the desire to better understand and accept myself and others despite our human limitations.

WEEK / • /	Monday	Tuesday
	NOTES	
Students of Concern This Week		
Things to Do This Week		

☐ DO √ DONE ✕ DISMISS ▲ DELEGATE ▶ DEFER

TAKE A MINUTE

Jot down some insights and ideas about what you can do in response to your scores on the previous page. To learn more about the Six Dimensions of Wellness and find some useful tools and strategies, visit nationalwellness.org/tools.

Visit www.mindtools.com/pages/article/HALT-risk-states.html

THE HALT CHECKLIST

Hungry	Angry
Why are you hungry?	Why are you angry?
Are you bored?	Is it stress? Anxiety?
Are you dehydrated?	Who/what would help?

Lonely	Tired
Why are you feeling this?	How much are you sleeping?
Online too much/too long?	Are you physically or emotionally tired?
Who can you connect with?	What is your sleep routine?

Wednesday	Thursday	Friday
NOTES		

CHECK UP AND CHECK IN

Take time to evaluate your mental and emotional health this week; then use the space to the right to reflect on your self-evaluation and the reasons you are feeling as you do this week.

IN CRISIS	STRUGGLING	SURVIVING	THRIVING	EXCELLING
Very anxious	Anxious	Worried	Positive	Cheerful
Very low mood	Depressed	Nervous	Calm	Joyful
Absenteeism	Tired	Irritable	Performing	Energetic
Exhausted	Poor performance	Sad	Sleeping well	High performance
Very poor sleep	Poor sleep	Trouble sleeping	Eating normally	Flow
Weight loss	Poor appetite	Distracted	Normal social activity	Fully realizing potential
		Withdrawn		

WEEK

/ • /

Students of Concern This Week

Things to Do This Week

	Monday	Tuesday
NOTES		

☐ DO ✓ DONE ✗ DISMISS ▲ DELEGATE ▶ DEFER

158

_____
_____
_____
_____
_____
_____
_____
_____
_____
_____
_____

THE EMPATHY MAP

SAYS	**THINKS**
What someone says about a situation, a person, an experience.	What someone thinks about something (but may not actually say).

WHAT THE PERSON

DOES	**FEELS**
How someone acts in response to people, a place, a situation, or experience.	What someone feels in response to a person, event, experience, or place.

Visit www.nngroup.com/artides/empathy-mapping/

Wednesday	Thursday	Friday
NOTES		

MY PERSONAL SIDE

1 **CONTENTMENT:** I felt good about things in general this week.

          never   rarely   sometimes   usually   always

2 **CONNECTION:** I felt connected to my friends, family, community, and interests this week.

          never   rarely   sometimes   usually   always

3 **CONDITION:** I felt physically, mentally, and spiritually/existentially healthy this week.

          never   rarely   sometimes   usually   always

4 **COMMITMENTS:** I met all of my obligations to myself and others this week.

          never   rarely   sometimes   usually   always

5 **CONTROL:** I felt like I was in control of my life and its demands this week.

          never   rarely   sometimes   usually   always

6 **CONCERNS:** This week, my most urgent personal concerns are:

WEEK

/ • /

Students of Concern This Week

Things to Do This Week

	Monday	Tuesday
	NOTES	

☐ DO   √ DONE   ✕ DISMISS   ▲ DELEGATE   ▶ DEFER

MY PROFESSIONAL SIDE

1 **COMMITMENT:** My commitment and connection to my students and their learning was evident. **never rarely sometimes usually always**

2 **CREDIBILITY:** My teaching reinforced or improved my credibility with my students and colleagues. **never rarely sometimes usually always**

3 **CLARITY:** I made clear each day what students were learning and how they knew they learned it. **never rarely sometimes usually always**

4 **CULTURE:** All of my students felt known, respected, safe, and engaged while in my classroom. **never rarely sometimes usually always**

5 **CONTRIBUTIONS:** I made substantive contributions to my school, department, team, or profession. **never rarely sometimes usually always**

6 **CONCERNS:** This week, my most urgent professional concerns are:

INVITING CLASSROOMS

RESPECT Does each person feel a sense of agency and feel valued by others?	**TRUST** Is it safe to take risks, to assume others' positive intentions and mutual investment?
OPTIMISM Does everyone believe others have untapped potential and can learn and succeed with proper support?	**INTENTIONALITY** Do all people, places, policies, programs, and processes foster feelings of trust, respect, and optimism?

Purkey, William. "Creating Safe Schools Through Invitational Education."

Wednesday	Thursday	Friday
NOTES		

JUST CHECKING! THE SIX DIMENSIONS OF WELLNESS

1 **CONTENTMENT:** I felt good about things in general this week.

                never   rarely   sometimes   usually   always

2 **CONNECTION:** I felt connected to my friends, family, community, and interests this week.

                never   rarely   sometimes   usually   always

3 **CONDITION:** I felt physically, mentally, and spiritually/existentially healthy this week.

                never   rarely   sometimes   usually   always

4 **COMMITMENTS:** I met all of my obligations to myself and others this week.

                never   rarely   sometimes   usually   always

5 **CONTROL:** I felt like I was in control of my life and its demands this week.

                never   rarely   sometimes   usually   always

6 **CONCERNS:** This week, my most urgent personal concerns are:

WEEK	Monday	Tuesday
/ • /	NOTES	
Students of Concern This Week		
Things to Do This Week		

□ DO √ DONE ✗ DISMISS ▲ DELEGATE ▶ DEFER

162

TAKE A MINUTE

1 **COMMITMENT:** My commitment and connection to my students and their learning
was evident.　　**never**　　**rarely**　　**sometimes**　　**usually**　　**always**

2 **CREDIBILITY:** My teaching reinforced or improved my credibility with my students and
colleagues.　　**never**　　**rarely**　　**sometimes**　　**usually**　　**always**

3 **CLARITY:** I made clear each day what students were learning and how they knew they
learned it.　　**never**　　**rarely**　　**sometimes**　　**usually**　　**always**

4 **CULTURE:** All of my students felt known, respected, safe, and engaged while in my
classroom.　　**never**　　**rarely**　　**sometimes**　　**usually**　　**always**

5 **CONTRIBUTIONS:** I made substantive contributions to my school, department, team,
or profession.　　**never**　　**rarely**　　**sometimes**　　**usually**　　**always**

6 **CONCERNS:** This week, my most urgent professional concerns are:

THE PDSA CYCLE

PLAN	DO
Create a plan, method, or process to test a possible strategy for improving teaching/ learning.	Test your plan, method, or process; collect data to refine or improve the plan/method.
ACT	**STUDY**
Based on the data, implement, improve, or replace strategy or approach with new one.	Analyse results to identify key insights about what to refine or change to improve the strategy or approach.

Visit deming.org/explore/pdsa/ for more information on the
PDSA Cycle

Wednesday	Thursday	Friday

CHECK UP AND CHECK IN

Take time to evaluate your mental and emotional health this week; then use the space to the right to reflect on your self-evaluation and the reasons you are feeling as you do this week.

IN CRISIS	STRUGGLING	SURVIVING	THRIVING	EXCELLING
Very anxious	Anxious	Worried	Positive	Cheerful
Very low mood	Depressed	Nervous	Calm	Joyful
Absenteeism	Tired	Irritable	Performing	Energetic
Exhausted	Poor performance	Sad	Sleeping well	High performance
Very poor sleep	Poor sleep	Trouble sleeping	Eating normally	Flow
Weight loss	Poor appetite	Distracted	Normal social activity	Fully realizing potential
		Withdrawn		

WEEK

/ • /

Students of Concern This Week

Things to Do This Week

	Monday	Tuesday
NOTES		

☐ DO √ DONE ✕ DISMISS ▲ DELEGATE ▶ DEFER

ACADEMIC	CULTURAL
What skills and strategies can students use to handle these cognitively demanding tasks?	What knowledge of past/present events do students need to consider? Are there connections to one's culture?
SOCIAL	EMOTIONAL
How can I help students navigate different settings, viewpoints, and needs when communicating ideas?	What emotions does this arouse and how can one learn to manage such feelings and beliefs?

Teaching Reading to Black Adolescent Males: Closing the Achievement Gap,
Alfred Tatum (2005, 35)

Wednesday	Thursday	Friday
NOTES		

NOTES

Use this page to jot down notes from the past six weeks to help you understand what you got right, what you still wonder, and what you need to keep working on or learning more about.

NOTES

Use this page to jot down notes based on the past six weeks to help you understand what you can do to improve in the key areas you have identified as important this year.

MY PERSONAL SIDE

1 **CONTENTMENT:** I felt good about things in general this week.

            never   rarely   sometimes   usually   always

2 **CONNECTION:** I felt connected to my friends, family, community, and interests this week.

            never   rarely   sometimes   usually   always

3 **CONDITION:** I felt physically, mentally, and spiritually/existentially healthy this week.

            never   rarely   sometimes   usually   always

4 **COMMITMENTS:** I met all of my obligations to myself and others this week.

            never   rarely   sometimes   usually   always

5 **CONTROL:** I felt like I was in control of my life and its demands this week.

            never   rarely   sometimes   usually   always

6 **CONCERNS:** This week, my most urgent personal concerns are:

WEEK / . /	Monday	Tuesday
	NOTES	
Students of Concern This Week		
Things to Do This Week		

□ DO ✓ DONE ✗ DISMISS ▲ DELEGATE ▶ DEFER

MY PROFESSIONAL SIDE

1 **COMMITMENT:** My commitment and connection to my students and their learning was
   evident.   **never**   **rarely**   **sometimes**   **usually**   **always**

2 **CREDIBILITY:** My teaching reinforced or improved my credibility with my students and
   colleagues.   **never**   **rarely**   **sometimes**   **usually**   **always**

3 **CLARITY:** I made clear each day what students were learning and how they knew they
   learned it.   **never**   **rarely**   **sometimes**   **usually**   **always**

4 **CULTURE:** All of my students felt known, respected, safe, and engaged while in my
   classroom.   **never**   **rarely**   **sometimes**   **usually**   **always**

5 **CONTRIBUTIONS:** I made substantive contributions to my school, department, team,
   or profession.   **never**   **rarely**   **sometimes**   **usually**   **always**

6 **CONCERNS:** This week, my most urgent professional concerns are:

THE EISENHOWER MATRIX

	URGENT	NOT URGENT
IMPORTANT	**DO** Do it now	**DECIDE** Specifically when to do it
UNIMPORTANT	**DELEGATE** Ask someone else	**DELETE** Do not do it

Visit eisenhower.me/eisenhower-matrix/
for more information

Wednesday	Thursday	Friday
NOTES		

JUST CHECKING! THE SIX DIMENSIONS OF WELLNESS

Complete this brief inventory to evaluate your wellbeing; then follow the directions on the page to the right.

1 _____ **OCCUPATIONAL:** Despite the inevitable challenges, I am finding my work rewarding and energizing because it offers me a chance to use and develop my knowledge and talents to help my students and colleagues.

2 _____ **PHYSICAL:** Though I had many obligations and demands on my time and energy, I made an effort to maintain a healthy diet, get enough sleep, and exercise to feel well.

3 _____ **SOCIAL:** I had a lot going on this week, but I made time to connect with colleagues and kids, friends and family so that I could contribute to my community and enjoy the relationships I have with people important to me.

4 _____ **INTELLECTUAL:** Yes, I had many responsibilities this week, but I made a point of learning new things that allowed me to deepen my knowledge and improve my skills so that I could identify and solve challenging problems.

5 _____ **SPIRITUAL:** Throughout the week, I have often felt overwhelmed; however, I carved out time to feel and express my gratitude, as well as to think about and act in accordance with my values and beliefs.

6 _____ **EMOTIONAL:** As I navigated the many obstacles I encountered this week, I listened to what I and others felt, guided by the desire to better understand and accept myself and others despite our human limitations.

WEEK ___ / ___ . ___ / ___	Monday	Tuesday
	NOTES	
Students of Concern This Week		
Things to Do This Week		

☐ DO √ DONE ✕ DISMISS ▲ DELEGATE ▶ DEFER

TAKE A MINUTE

Jot down some insights and ideas about what you can do in response to your scores on the previous page. To learn more about the Six Dimensions of Wellness and find some useful tools and strategies, visit nationalwellness.org/tools.

_____

_____

_____

_____

_____

_____

THE HALT CHECKLIST

Hungry	**Angry**
Why are you hungry?	Why are you angry?
Are you bored?	Is it stress? Anxiety?
Are you dehydrated?	Who/what would help?
Lonely	**Tired**
Why are you feeling this?	How much are you sleeping?
Online too much/too long?	Are you physically or emotionally tired?
Who can you connect with?	What is your sleep routine?

Visit www.mindtools.com/pages/article/HALT-risk-states.html

Wednesday	Thursday	Friday
NOTES		

CHECK UP AND CHECK IN

Take time to evaluate your mental and emotional health this week; then use the space to the right to reflect on your self-evaluation and the reasons you are feeling as you do this week.

IN CRISIS	STRUGGLING	SURVIVING	THRIVING	EXCELLING
Very anxious	Anxious	Worried	Positive	Cheerful
Very low mood	Depressed	Nervous	Calm	Joyful
Absenteeism	Tired	Irritable	Performing	Energetic
Exhausted	Poor performance	Sad	Sleeping well	High performance
Very poor sleep	Poor sleep	Trouble sleeping	Eating normally	Flow
Weight loss	Poor appetite	Distracted	Normal social activity	Fully realizing potential
		Withdrawn		

WEEK

/ . /

Students of Concern This Week

Things to Do This Week

	Monday	Tuesday
NOTES		

□ DO √ DONE ✗ DISMISS ▲ DELEGATE ▶ DEFER

_____
_____
_____
_____
_____
_____
_____
_____
_____
_____
_____
_____
_____

THE EMPATHY MAP

SAYS	**THINKS**
What someone says about a situation, a person, an experience.	What someone thinks about something (but may not actually say).

WHAT THE PERSON

DOES	**FEELS**
How someone acts in response to people, a place, a situation, or experience.	What someone feels in response to a person, event, experience, or place.

Visit www.nngroup.com/artides/empathy-mapping/

Wednesday	Thursday	Friday
NOTES		

MY PERSONAL SIDE

1 **CONTENTMENT:** I felt good about things in general this week.

                never   rarely   sometimes   usually   always

2 **CONNECTION:** I felt connected to my friends, family, community, and interests this week.

                never   rarely   sometimes   usually   always

3 **CONDITION:** I felt physically, mentally, and spiritually/existentially healthy this week.

                never   rarely   sometimes   usually   always

4 **COMMITMENTS:** I met all of my obligations to myself and others this week.

                never   rarely   sometimes   usually   always

5 **CONTROL:** I felt like I was in control of my life and its demands this week.

                never   rarely   sometimes   usually   always

6 **CONCERNS:** This week, my most urgent personal concerns are:

WEEK	Monday	Tuesday
/ . /	NOTES	
Students of Concern This Week		
Things to Do This Week		

☐ DO √ DONE ✕ DISMISS ▲ DELEGATE ▶ DEFER

174

MY PROFESSIONAL SIDE

1 **COMMITMENT:** My commitment and connection to my students and their learning was evident.   **never**   **rarely**   **sometimes**   **usually**   **always**

2 **CREDIBILITY:** My teaching reinforced or improved my credibility with my students and colleagues.   **never**   **rarely**   **sometimes**   **usually**   **always**

3 **CLARITY:** I made clear each day what students were learning and how they knew they learned it.   **never**   **rarely**   **sometimes**   **usually**   **always**

4 **CULTURE:** All of my students felt known, respected, safe, and engaged while in my classroom.   **never**   **rarely**   **sometimes**   **usually**   **always**

5 **CONTRIBUTIONS:** I made substantive contributions to my school, department, team, or profession.   **never**   **rarely**   **sometimes**   **usually**   **always**

6 **CONCERNS:** This week, my most urgent professional concerns are:

INVITING CLASSROOMS

RESPECT Does each person feel a sense of agency and feel valued by others?	**TRUST** Is it safe to take risks, to assume others' positive intentions and mutual investment?
OPTIMISM Does everyone believe others have untapped potential and can learn and succeed with proper support?	**INTENTIONALITY** Do all people, places, policies, programs, and processes foster feelings of trust, respect, and optimism?

Purkey, William. "Creating Safe Schools Through Invitational Education."

Wednesday	Thursday	Friday
NOTES		

JUST CHECKING! THE SIX DIMENSIONS OF WELLNESS

1 **CONTENTMENT:** I felt good about things in general this week.

                never   rarely   sometimes   usually   always

2 **CONNECTION:** I felt connected to my friends, family, community, and interests this week.

                never   rarely   sometimes   usually   always

3 **CONDITION:** I felt physically, mentally, and spiritually/existentially healthy this week.

                never   rarely   sometimes   usually   always

4 **COMMITMENTS:** I met all of my obligations to myself and others this week.

                never   rarely   sometimes   usually   always

5 **CONTROL:** I felt like I was in control of my life and its demands this week.

                never   rarely   sometimes   usually   always

6 **CONCERNS:** This week, my most urgent personal concerns are:

WEEK	Monday	Tuesday
/ . /	NOTES	
Students of Concern This Week		
Things to Do This Week		

□ DO √ DONE ✗ DISMISS ▲ DELEGATE ▶ DEFER

TAKE A MINUTE

1 **COMMITMENT:** My commitment and connection to my students and their learning was evident.   **never**   **rarely**   **sometimes**   **usually**   **always**

2 **CREDIBILITY:** My teaching reinforced or improved my credibility with my students and colleagues.   **never**   **rarely**   **sometimes**   **usually**   **always**

3 **CLARITY:** I made clear each day what students were learning and how they knew they learned it.   **never**   **rarely**   **sometimes**   **usually**   **always**

4 **CULTURE:** All of my students felt known, respected, safe, and engaged while in my classroom.   **never**   **rarely**   **sometimes**   **usually**   **always**

5 **CONTRIBUTIONS:** I made substantive contributions to my school, department, team, or profession.   **never**   **rarely**   **sometimes**   **usually**   **always**

6 **CONCERNS:** This week, my most urgent professional concerns are:

THE PDSA CYCLE

PLAN	DO
Create a plan, method, or process to test a possible strategy for improving teaching/learning.	Test your plan, method, or process; collect data to refine or improve the plan/method.
ACT	**STUDY**
Based on the data, implement, improve, or replace strategy or approach with new one.	Analyse results to identify key insights about what to refine or change to improve the strategy or approach.

Visit deming.org/explore/pdsa/ for more information on the PDSA Cycle

Wednesday	Thursday	Friday
NOTES		

CHECK UP AND CHECK IN

Take time to evaluate your mental and emotional health this week; then use the space to the right to reflect on your self-evaluation and the reasons you are feeling as you do this week.

IN CRISIS	STRUGGLING	SURVIVING	THRIVING	EXCELLING
Very anxious	Anxious	Worried	Positive	Cheerful
Very low mood	Depressed	Nervous	Calm	Joyful
Absenteeism	Tired	Irritable	Performing	Energetic
Exhausted	Poor performance	Sad	Sleeping well	High performance
Very poor sleep	Poor sleep	Trouble sleeping	Eating normally	Flow
Weight loss	Poor appetite	Distracted	Normal social activity	Fully realizing potential
		Withdrawn		

WEEK

/ . /

Students of Concern This Week

Things to Do This Week

☐ DO √ DONE ✗ DISMISS ▲ DELEGATE ▶ DEFER

	Monday	Tuesday
NOTES		

ACADEMIC	CULTURAL
What skills and strategies can students use to handle these cognitively demanding tasks?	What knowledge of past/present events do students need to consider? Are there connections to one's culture?
SOCIAL	**EMOTIONAL**
How can I help students navigate different settings, viewpoints, and needs when communicating ideas?	What emotions does this arouse and how can one learn to manage such feelings and beliefs?

Teaching Reading to Black Adolescent Males: Closing the Achievement Gap,
Alfred Tatum (2005, 35)

Wednesday	Thursday	Friday
Notes		

NOTES

Use this page to jot down notes from the past six weeks to help you understand what you got right, what you still wonder, and what you need to keep working on or learning more about.

NOTES

Use this page to jot down notes based on the past six weeks to help you understand what you can do to improve in the key areas you have identified as important this year.

MY PERSONAL SIDE

1 **CONTENTMENT:** I felt good about things in general this week.

　　　　　　　never　　　rarely　　　sometimes　　　usually　　　always

2 **CONNECTION:** I felt connected to my friends, family, community, and interests this week.

　　　　　　　never　　　rarely　　　sometimes　　　usually　　　always

3 **CONDITION:** I felt physically, mentally, and spiritually/existentially healthy this week.

　　　　　　　never　　　rarely　　　sometimes　　　usually　　　always

4 **COMMITMENTS:** I met all of my obligations to myself and others this week.

　　　　　　　never　　　rarely　　　sometimes　　　usually　　　always

5 **CONTROL:** I felt like I was in control of my life and its demands this week.

　　　　　　　never　　　rarely　　　sometimes　　　usually　　　always

6 **CONCERNS:** This week, my most urgent personal concerns are:

WEEK	Monday	Tuesday
/ ． /	NOTES	
Students of Concern This Week		

Things to Do This Week

□ DO　√ DONE　✕ DISMISS　▲ DELEGATE　▶ DEFER

MY PROFESSIONAL SIDE

1 **COMMITMENT:** My commitment and connection to my students and their learning was
   evident.   **never**   **rarely**   **sometimes**   **usually**   **always**

2 **CREDIBILITY:** My teaching reinforced or improved my credibility with my students and
   colleagues.   **never**   **rarely**   **sometimes**   **usually**   **always**

3 **CLARITY:** I made clear each day what students were learning and how they knew they
   learned it.   **never**   **rarely**   **sometimes**   **usually**   **always**

4 **CULTURE:** All of my students felt known, respected, safe, and engaged while in my
   classroom.   **never**   **rarely**   **sometimes**   **usually**   **always**

5 **CONTRIBUTIONS:** I made substantive contributions to my school, department, team, or
   profession.   **never**   **rarely**   **sometimes**   **usually**   **always**

6 **CONCERNS:** This week, my most urgent professional concerns are:

THE EISENHOWER MATRIX

	URGENT	NOT URGENT
IMPORTANT	**DO** Do it now	**DECIDE** Specifically when to do it
UNIMPORTANT	**DELEGATE** Ask someone else	**DELETE** Do not do it

Visit eisenhower.me/eisenhower-matrix/
for more information

Wednesday	Thursday	Friday
NOTES		

JUST CHECKING! THE SIX DIMENSIONS OF WELLNESS

Complete this brief inventory to evaluate your wellbeing; then follow the directions on the page to the right.

1 _____ **OCCUPATIONAL:** Despite the inevitable challenges, I am finding my work rewarding and energizing because it offers me a chance to use and develop my knowledge and talents to help my students and colleagues.

2 _____ **PHYSICAL:** Though I had many obligations and demands on my time and energy, I made an effort to maintain a healthy diet, get enough sleep, and exercise to feel well.

3 _____ **SOCIAL:** I had a lot going on this week, but I made time to connect with colleagues and kids, friends and family so that I could contribute to my community and enjoy the relationships I have with people important to me.

4 _____ **INTELLECTUAL:** Yes, I had many responsibilities this week, but I made a point of learning new things that allowed me to deepen my knowledge and improve my skills so that I could identify and solve challenging problems.

5 _____ **SPIRITUAL:** Throughout the week, I have often felt overwhelmed; however, I carved out time to feel and express my gratitude, as well as to think about and act in accordance with my values and beliefs.

6 _____ **EMOTIONAL:** As I navigated the many obstacles I encountered this week, I listened to what I and others felt, guided by the desire to better understand and accept myself and others despite our human limitations.

WEEK / . /	Monday	Tuesday
	NOTES	

Students of Concern This Week

Things to Do This Week

☐ DO √ DONE ✗ DISMISS ▲ DELEGATE ▶ DEFER

TAKE A MINUTE

Jot down some insights and ideas about what you can do in response to your scores on the previous page. To learn more about the Six Dimensions of Wellness and find some useful tools and strategies, visit nationalwellness.org/tools.

_____

_____

_____

_____

_____

_____

THE HALT CHECKLIST

Hungry	**Angry**
Why are you hungry?	Why are you angry?
Are you bored?	Is it stress? Anxiety?
Are you dehydrated?	Who/what would help?
Lonely	**Tired**
Why are you feeling this?	How much are you sleeping?
Online too much/too long?	Are you physically or emotionally tired?
Who can you connect with?	What is your sleep routine?

Visit www.mindtools.com/pages/article/HALT-risk-states.html

Wednesday	Thursday	Friday
NOTES		

CHECK UP AND CHECK IN

Take time to evaluate your mental and emotional health this week; then use the space to the right to reflect on your self-evaluation and the reasons you are feeling as you do this week.

IN CRISIS	STRUGGLING	SURVIVING	THRIVING	EXCELLING
Very anxious	Anxious	Wworried	Positive	Cheerful
Very low mood	Depressed	Nervous	Calm	Joyful
Absenteeism	Tired	Irritable	Performing	Energetic
Exhausted	Poor performance	Sad	Sleeping well	High performance
Very poor sleep	Poor sleep	Trouble sleeping	Eating normally	Flow
Weight loss	Poor appetite	Distracted	Normal social activity	Fully realizing potential
		Withdrawn		

WEEK

_____ / _____ • _____ / _____

Students of Concern This Week

Things to Do This Week

	Monday	Tuesday
NOTES		

☐ DO √ DONE ✕ DISMISS ▲ DELEGATE ▶ DEFER

THE EMPATHY MAP

SAYS	THINKS
What someone says about a situation, a person, an experience.	What someone thinks about something (but may not actually say).

WHAT THE PERSON

DOES	FEELS
How someone acts in response to people, a place, a situation, or experience.	What someone feels in response to a person, event, experience, or place.

Visit www.nngroup.com/artides/empathy-mapping/

Wednesday	Thursday	Friday
NOTES		

MY PERSONAL SIDE

1 **CONTENTMENT:** I felt good about things in general this week.

        never   rarely   sometimes   usually   always

2 **CONNECTION:** I felt connected to my friends, family, community, and interests this week.

        never   rarely   sometimes   usually   always

3 **CONDITION:** I felt physically, mentally, and spiritually/existentially healthy this week.

        never   rarely   sometimes   usually   always

4 **COMMITMENTS:** I met all of my obligations to myself and others this week.

        never   rarely   sometimes   usually   always

5 **CONTROL:** I felt like I was in control of my life and its demands this week.

        never   rarely   sometimes   usually   always

6 **CONCERNS:** This week, my most urgent personal concerns are:

WEEK / . /	Monday	Tuesday
	NOTES	

Students of Concern This Week

Things to Do This Week

☐ DO √ DONE ✗ DISMISS ▲ DELEGATE ▶ DEFER

MY PROFESSIONAL SIDE

1 **COMMITMENT:** My commitment and connection to my students and their learning was evident.   **never**   **rarely**   **sometimes**   **usually**   **always**

2 **CREDIBILITY:** My teaching reinforced or improved my credibility with my students and colleagues.   **never**   **rarely**   **sometimes**   **usually**   **always**

3 **CLARITY:** I made clear each day what students were learning and how they knew they learned it.   **never**   **rarely**   **sometimes**   **usually**   **always**

4 **CULTURE:** All of my students felt known, respected, safe, and engaged while in my classroom.   **never**   **rarely**   **sometimes**   **usually**   **always**

5 **CONTRIBUTIONS:** I made substantive contributions to my school, department, team, or profession.   **never**   **rarely**   **sometimes**   **usually**   **always**

6 **CONCERNS:** This week, my most urgent professional concerns are:

RESPECT Does each person feel a sense of agency and feel valued by others?	**TRUST** Is it safe to take risks, to assume others' positive intentions and mutual investment?
OPTIMISM Does everyone believe others have untapped potential and can learn and succeed with proper support?	**INTENTIONALITY** Do all people, places, policies, programs, and processes foster feelings of trust, respect, and optimism?

Purkey, William. "Creating Safe Schools Through Invitational Education."

Wednesday	Thursday	Friday
NOTES		

JUST CHECKING! THE SIX DIMENSIONS OF WELLNESS

1 **CONTENTMENT:** I felt good about things in general this week.

           never   **rarely**   **sometimes**   **usually**   **always**

2 **CONNECTION:** I felt connected to my friends, family, community, and interests this week.

           never   **rarely**   **sometimes**   **usually**   **always**

3 **CONDITION:** I felt physically, mentally, and spiritually/existentially healthy this week.

           never   **rarely**   **sometimes**   **usually**   **always**

4 **COMMITMENTS:** I met all of my obligations to myself and others this week.

           never   **rarely**   **sometimes**   **usually**   **always**

5 **CONTROL:** I felt like I was in control of my life and its demands this week.

           never   **rarely**   **sometimes**   **usually**   **always**

6 **CONCERNS:** This week, my most urgent personal concerns are:

WEEK		Monday	Tuesday
		NOTES	
/ . /			
Students of Concern This Week			

Things to Do This Week

☐ DO √ DONE ✗ DISMISS ▲ DELEGATE ▶ DEFER

TAKE A MINUTE

1 **COMMITMENT:** My commitment and connection to my students and their learning was evident. **never** **rarely** **sometimes** **usually** **always**

2 **CREDIBILITY:** My teaching reinforced or improved my credibility with my students and colleagues. **never** **rarely** **sometimes** **usually** **always**

3 **CLARITY:** I made clear each day what students were learning and how they knew they learned it. **never** **rarely** **sometimes** **usually** **always**

4 **CULTURE:** All of my students felt known, respected, safe, and engaged while in my classroom. **never** **rarely** **sometimes** **usually** **always**

5 **CONTRIBUTIONS:** I made substantive contributions to my school, department, team, or profession. **never** **rarely** **sometimes** **usually** **always**

6 **CONCERNS:** This week, my most urgent professional concerns are:

THE PDSA CYCLE

PLAN	DO
Create a plan, method, or process to test a possible strategy for improving teaching/ learning.	Test your plan, method, or process; collect data to refine or improve the plan/method.
ACT	**STUDY**
Based on the data, implement, improve, or replace strategy or approach with new one.	Analyse results to identify key insights about what to refine or change to improve the strategy or approach.

Visit deming.org/explore/pdsa/ for more information on the PDSA Cycle

Wednesday	Thursday	Friday

191

CHECK UP AND CHECK IN

Take time to evaluate your mental and emotional health this week; then use the space to the right to reflect on your self-evaluation and the reasons you are feeling as you do this week.

IN CRISIS	STRUGGLING	SURVIVING	THRIVING	EXCELLING
Very anxious	Anxious	Worried	Positive	Cheerful
Very low mood	Depressed	Nervous	Calm	Joyful
Absenteeism	Tired	Irritable	Performing	Energetic
Exhausted	Poor performance	Sad	Sleeping well	High performance
Very poor sleep	Poor sleep	Trouble sleeping	Eating normally	Flow
Weight loss	Poor appetite	Distracted	Normal social activity	Fully realizing potential
		Withdrawn		

WEEK

___ / ___ . ___ / ___

Students of Concern This Week

Things to Do This Week

	Monday	Tuesday
NOTES		

ACADEMIC	CULTURAL
What skills and strategies can students use to handle these cognitively demanding tasks?	What knowledge of past/present events do students need to consider? Are there connections to one's culture?
SOCIAL	EMOTIONAL
How can I help students navigate different settings, viewpoints, and needs when communicating ideas?	What emotions does this arouse and how can one learn to manage such feelings and beliefs?

Teaching Reading to Black Adolescent Males: Closing the Achievement Gap,
Alfred Tatum (2005, 35)

Wednesday	Thursday	Friday
NOTES		

NOTES

Use this page to jot down notes from the past six weeks to help you understand what you got right, what you still wonder, and what you need to keep working on or learning more about.

NOTES

Use this page to jot down notes based on the past six weeks to help you understand what you can do to improve in the key areas you have identified as important this year.

MY PERSONAL SIDE

1 **CONTENTMENT:** I felt good about things in general this week.

   never   rarely   sometimes   usually   always

2 **CONNECTION:** I felt connected to my friends, family, community, and interests this week.

   never   rarely   sometimes   usually   always

3 **CONDITION:** I felt physically, mentally, and spiritually/existentially healthy this week.

   never   rarely   sometimes   usually   always

4 **COMMITMENTS:** I met all of my obligations to myself and others this week.

   never   rarely   sometimes   usually   always

5 **CONTROL:** I felt like I was in control of my life and its demands this week.

   never   rarely   sometimes   usually   always

6 **CONCERNS:** This week, my most urgent personal concerns are:

WEEK	Monday	Tuesday
/ . /	NOTES	
Students of Concern This Week		
Things to Do This Week		

☐ DO   √ DONE   ✕ DISMISS   ▲ DELEGATE   ▶ DEFER

MY PROFESSIONAL SIDE

1 **COMMITMENT:** My commitment and connection to my students and their learning was evident.   **never   rarely   sometimes   usually   always**

2 **CREDIBILITY:** My teaching reinforced or improved my credibility with my students and colleagues.   **never   rarely   sometimes   usually   always**

3 **CLARITY:** I made clear each day what students were learning and how they knew they learned it.   **never   rarely   sometimes   usually   always**

4 **CULTURE:** All of my students felt known, respected, safe, and engaged while in my classroom.   **never   rarely   sometimes   usually   always**

5 **CONTRIBUTIONS:** I made substantive contributions to my school, department, team, or profession.   **never   rarely   sometimes   usually   always**

6 **CONCERNS:** This week, my most urgent professional concerns are:

THE EISENHOWER MATRIX

	URGENT	NOT URGENT
IMPORTANT	**DO** Do it now	**DECIDE** Specifically when to do it
UNIMPORTANT	**DELEGATE** Ask someone else	**DELETE** Do not do it

Visit eisenhower.me/eisenhower-matrix/ for more information

Wednesday	Thursday	Friday
NOTES		

JUST CHECKING! THE SIX DIMENSIONS OF WELLNESS

Complete this brief inventory to evaluate your wellbeing; then follow the directions on the page to the right.

1 _____ **OCCUPATIONAL:** Despite the inevitable challenges, I am finding my work rewarding and energizing because it offers me a chance to use and develop my knowledge and talents to help my students and colleagues.

2 _____ **PHYSICAL:** Though I had many obligations and demands on my time and energy, I made an effort to maintain a healthy diet, get enough sleep, and exercise to feel well.

3 _____ **SOCIAL:** I had a lot going on this week, but I made time to connect with colleagues and kids, friends and family so that I could contribute to my community and enjoy the relationships I have with people important to me.

4 _____ **INTELLECTUAL:** Yes, I had many responsibilities this week, but I made a point of learning new things that allowed me to deepen my knowledge and improve my skills so that I could identify and solve challenging problems.

5 _____ **SPIRITUAL:** Throughout the week, I have often felt overwhelmed; however, I carved out time to feel and express my gratitude, as well as to think about and act in accordance with my values and beliefs.

6 _____ **EMOTIONAL:** As I navigated the many obstacles I encountered this week, I listened to what I and others felt, guided by the desire to better understand and accept myself and others despite our human limitations.

WEEK / . /	Monday	Tuesday
	NOTES	
Students of Concern This Week		
Things to Do This Week		

☐ DO √ DONE ✕ DISMISS ▲ DELEGATE ▶ DEFER

TAKE A MINUTE

Jot down some insights and ideas about what you can do in response to your scores on the previous page. To learn more about the Six Dimensions of Wellness and find some useful tools and strategies, visit nationalwellness.org/tools.

_____

_____

_____

_____

_____

_____

THE HALT CHECKLIST

Hungry	**Angry**
Why are you hungry?	Why are you angry?
Are you bored?	Is it stress? Anxiety?
Are you dehydrated?	Who/what would help?
Lonely	**Tired**
Why are you feeling this?	How much are you sleeping?
Online too much/too long?	Are you physically or emotionally tired?
Who can you connect with?	What is your sleep routine?

Visit www.mindtools.com/pages/article/HALT-risk-states.html

Wednesday	Thursday	Friday

CHECK UP AND CHECK IN

Take time to evaluate your mental and emotional health this week; then use the space to the right to reflect on your self-evaluation and the reasons you are feeling as you do this week.

IN CRISIS	STRUGGLING	SURVIVING	THRIVING	EXCELLING
Very anxious	Anxious	Worried	Positive	Cheerful
Very low mood	Depressed	Nervous	Calm	Joyful
Absenteeism	Tired	Irritable	Performing	Energetic
Exhausted	Poor performance	Sad	Sleeping well	High performance
Very poor sleep	Poor sleep	Trouble sleeping	Eating normally	Flow
Weight loss	Poor appetite	Distracted	Normal social activity	Fully realizing potential
		Withdrawn		

WEEK

/ . /

Students of Concern This Week

Things to Do This Week

Monday	Tuesday
NOTES	

☐ DO √ DONE ✕ DISMISS ▲ DELEGATE ▶ DEFER

THE EMPATHY MAP

SAYS What someone says about a situation, a person, an experience.	**THINKS** What someone thinks about something (but may not actually say).

WHAT THE PERSON

DOES How someone acts in response to people, a place, a situation, or experience.	**FEELS** What someone feels in response to a person, event, experience, or place.

Visit www.nngroup.com/artides/empathy-mapping/

Wednesday	Thursday	Friday
NOTES		

MY PERSONAL SIDE

1 **CONTENTMENT:** I felt good about things in general this week.

        never   rarely   sometimes   usually   always

2 **CONNECTION:** I felt connected to my friends, family, community, and interests this week.

        never   rarely   sometimes   usually   always

3 **CONDITION:** I felt physically, mentally, and spiritually/existentially healthy this week.

        never   rarely   sometimes   usually   always

4 **COMMITMENTS:** I met all of my obligations to myself and others this week.

        never   rarely   sometimes   usually   always

5 **CONTROL:** I felt like I was in control of my life and its demands this week.

        never   rarely   sometimes   usually   always

6 **CONCERNS:** This week, my most urgent personal concerns are:

WEEK / . /	Monday	Tuesday
	NOTES	
Students of Concern This Week		
Things to Do This Week		

☐ DO   √ DONE   ✕ DISMISS   ▲ DELEGATE   ▶ DEFER

MY PROFESSIONAL SIDE

1 **COMMITMENT:** My commitment and connection to my students and their learning was evident.   never   rarely   sometimes   usually   always

2 **CREDIBILITY:** My teaching reinforced or improved my credibility with my students and colleagues.   never   rarely   sometimes   usually   always

3 **CLARITY:** I made clear each day what students were learning and how they knew they learned it.   never   rarely   sometimes   usually   always

4 **CULTURE:** All of my students felt known, respected, safe, and engaged while in my classroom.   never   rarely   sometimes   usually   always

5 **CONTRIBUTIONS:** I made substantive contributions to my school, department, team, or profession.   never   rarely   sometimes   usually   always

6 **CONCERNS:** This week, my most urgent professional concerns are:

INVITING CLASSROOMS

RESPECT Does each person feel a sense of agency and feel valued by others?	**TRUST** Is it safe to take risks, to assume others' positive intentions and mutual investment?
OPTIMISM Does everyone believe others have untapped potential and can learn and succeed with proper support?	**INTENTIONALITY** Do all people, places, policies, programs, and processes foster feelings of trust, respect, and optimism?

Purkey, William. "Creating Safe Schools Through Invitational Education."

Wednesday	Thursday	Friday

JUST CHECKING! THE SIX DIMENSIONS OF WELLNESS

1 **CONTENTMENT:** I felt good about things in general this week.

| never | rarely | sometimes | usually | always |

2 **CONNECTION:** I felt connected to my friends, family, community, and interests this week.

| never | rarely | sometimes | usually | always |

3 **CONDITION:** I felt physically, mentally, and spiritually/existentially healthy this week.

| never | rarely | sometimes | usually | always |

4 **COMMITMENTS:** I met all of my obligations to myself and others this week.

| never | rarely | sometimes | usually | always |

5 **CONTROL:** I felt like I was in control of my life and its demands this week.

| never | rarely | sometimes | usually | always |

6 **CONCERNS:** This week, my most urgent personal concerns are:

WEEK / . /	Monday	Tuesday
	NOTES	
Students of Concern This Week		
Things to Do This Week		

□ DO √ DONE ✗ DISMISS ▲ DELEGATE ▶ DEFER

TAKE A MINUTE

1 **COMMITMENT:** My commitment and connection to my students and their learning was evident. **never** **rarely** **sometimes** **usually** **always**

2 **CREDIBILITY:** My teaching reinforced or improved my credibility with my students and colleagues. **never** **rarely** **sometimes** **usually** **always**

3 **CLARITY:** I made clear each day what students were learning and how they knew they learned it. **never** **rarely** **sometimes** **usually** **always**

4 **CULTURE:** All of my students felt known, respected, safe, and engaged while in my classroom. **never** **rarely** **sometimes** **usually** **always**

5 **CONTRIBUTIONS:** I made substantive contributions to my school, department, team, or profession. **never** **rarely** **sometimes** **usually** **always**

6 **CONCERNS:** This week, my most urgent professional concerns are:

Wednesday	Thursday	Friday
NOTES		

CHECK UP AND CHECK IN

Take time to evaluate your mental and emotional health this week; then use the space to the right to reflect on your self-evaluation and the reasons you are feeling as you do this week.

IN CRISIS	STRUGGLING	SURVIVING	THRIVING	EXCELLING
Very anxious	Anxious	Worried	Positive	Cheerful
Very low mood	Depressed	Nervous	Calm	Joyful
Absenteeism	Tired	Irritable	Performing	Energetic
Exhausted	Poor performance	Sad	Sleeping well	High performance
Very poor sleep	Poor sleep	Trouble sleeping	Eating normally	Flow
Weight loss	Poor appetite	Distracted	Normal social activity	Fully realizing potential
		Withdrawn		

WEEK

/ . /

Students of Concern This Week

Things to Do This Week

	Monday	Tuesday
NOTES		

☐ DO √ DONE ✕ DISMISS ▲ DELEGATE ▶ DEFER

INCORPORATE MULTIPLE LITERACIES

ACADEMIC	CULTURAL
What skills and strategies can students use to handle these cognitively demanding tasks?	What knowledge of past/present events do students need to consider? Are there connections to one's culture?
SOCIAL	EMOTIONAL
How can I help students navigate different settings, viewpoints, and needs when communicating ideas?	What emotions does this arouse and how can one learn to manage such feelings and beliefs?

Teaching Reading to Black Adolescent Males: Closing the Achievement Gap,
Alfred Tatum (2005, 35)

Wednesday	Thursday	Friday
NOTES		

NOTES

Use this page to jot down notes from the past six weeks to help you understand what you got right, what you still wonder, and what you need to keep working on or learning more about.

NOTES

Use this page to jot down notes based on the past six weeks to help you understand what you can do to improve in the key areas you have identified as important this year.

THE **DAILY** PLAN SECTION

We fail to see, or refuse to accept, that any attempt to bring our ideas into concrete reality must inevitably fall short of our dreams, no matter how brilliantly we succeed in carrying things off—because reality, unlike fantasy, is a realm in which we don't have limitless control, and can't possibly hope to meet our perfectionist standards. Something—our limited talents, our limited time, our limited control over events, and over the actions of other people—will always render our creation less than perfect.

—**Oliver Burkeman**, *Four Thousand Weeks: Time Management for Mortals*

AGILE TEACHING: USING A DESIGN-THINKING PROCESS TO PLAN UNITS AND DAILY LESSONS

When teachers sit down to plan a unit or a create a lesson plan for the next day, we often do so with colleagues who teach the same class, working together in someone's classroom after school or collaborating later online by video chat or on a shared document we might be using the next day. If we have worked together on such a unit or lesson plan, and if we can count on having the time and opportunity, we will meet to debrief on what did and did not work, why, and for whom—and how we can improve this unit or lesson in the future. Such intentional teaching and analysis of the results, also known as "lesson study," leads to "gradual, incremental improvements in teaching over time [if we provide] clear learning goals for students, [and] a shared curriculum" (Stigler & Hiebert, 1999, p. 109).

Figure 1.1 The DIIE model

Evaluation: knowing the skills, having multiple methods, and collaboratively debating the magnitude of impact from the intervention.

Diagnosis and Discovery: using various assessment strategies to understand what each student brings to the lesson, including prior knowledge, motivations, and willingness to learn.

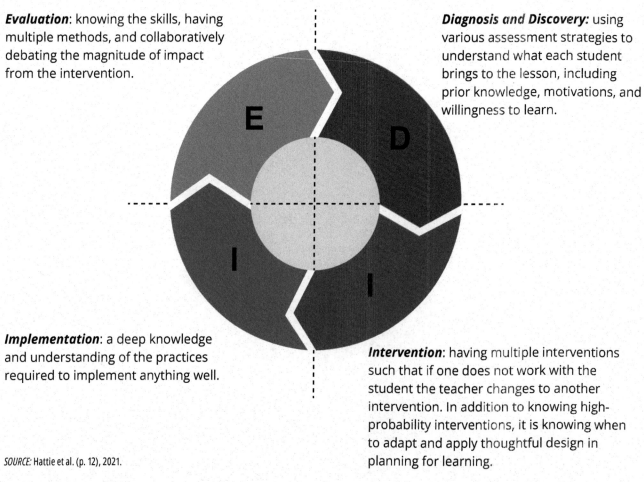

Implementation: a deep knowledge and understanding of the practices required to implement anything well.

Intervention: having multiple interventions such that if one does not work with the student the teacher changes to another intervention. In addition to knowing high-probability interventions, it is knowing when to adapt and apply thoughtful design in planning for learning.

SOURCE: Hattie et al. (p. 12), 2021.

Whether we are designing a multiweek unit or a specific lesson plan for a day, we will likely follow some version of a design-thinking process. Though there are many design-thinking models, they all share some common steps or principles:

1. **Seek first to understand your students**, *then* to be understood by them. The design-thinking process would refer to your students as "users"—of your lessons, texts, handouts, and anything else they must do or use to learn the intended lesson. This step in the process can be conducted through informal assessments, observations, questionnaires,

or interviews to clarify their understanding, skills, needs, level of engagement, or potential objections to the material you intend to teach.

2. **Define the problem** students are experiencing in a given area based on your investigations and insights from the previous step. In addition to the problem, try to understand the source of this difficulty and how it might be best addressed.

3. **Generate possible ideas** that would potentially help students learn or improve in the identified area(s) using texts, techniques, or teaching strategies that students will find engaging and challenging.

4. **Develop a viable prototype** of the unit or lesson that will address the problem you identified in the previous stages of the design process. The exact form of this prototype will inevitably depend on the class, subject area, and constraints within which you teach.

5. **Test it out with your students**, gathering information along the way about what does and does not work, for whom, and why.

6. **Use the data to refine, revise, or reject the prototype**, returning to the different ideas you generated in step 3 to improve the current prototype or develop a new one. Repeat the process as needed until you have a unit or assignment that achieves your intended outcome(s)—then move on to the next unit or lesson plan you need to design or refine.

Such a robust collaboration for designing and refining our units and lesson plans, however, is not representative of how all teachers work. Noting this irony, Dunn and Hattie (2022) observe that "the very idea of 'effective' teacher professional learning can be elusive, even within an industry that has learning at its core" (p. 3). Thus, for many, perhaps even most, teachers the design process unfolds when we are alone in our classrooms after school when we finally have time to think about what we will do the next day, or in a café on our way home from school, or at our kitchen table after dinner, or perhaps in our home office after we have put all the day's other demands (or even our children!) to bed and we can finally think about how to do our work just a bit better the next day.

Agile Design

As we have learned in recent years, things do not always go as we expected they would. Things happen, as the saying goes. Or as W. B. Yeats (1920) wrote, "Things fall apart; the centre cannot hold/Mere anarchy is loosed upon the world," and so, at school or at home, for our students or ourselves (or both), things can and often do go sideways or upside down. During such periods, planning amazing units and lesson plans is akin to carrying a sheet of plywood in a windstorm.

With this reality in mind, our units and lesson plans should be agile, able to accommodate sudden changes, unexpected results, or the untold disruptions that seem always poised to undermine our teaching. One year, for example, I carefully kept track of every minute that was taken from my instructional time for an entire year. It added up to almost *thirty hours* which, given that my periods at that time were fifty-one minutes long, amounted to more than a *month* of instructional time.

Design that prizes agility over efficiency allows us to take the time we need for students to learn if they need more time than we had anticipated; for students with special needs to get the accommodations required for their success; for all students to move from the inspiration point (mere engagement) to the perspiration point (learning of new material or methods) where they develop the academic identity and confidence that is an important goal of all the units and lessons we design. As Muhammad (2020) reminds us, we have other crucial goals to consider when designing our units and lessons: "We live in a period where there's no time for 'urgent-free' pedagogy. Our instructional pursuits must be honest, bold, raw, unapologetic, and responsive to the social times" (p. 54).

The concept of agile design has been around for some time in the software design field. Adapting the "Agile Manifesto" to designing units and lesson plans, we would arrive at something like this: Agile design is not overly dogmatic. If it works for you and your students, keep it, develop and improve it. If it doesn't fit your needs or those of your students, just be agile and drop it. Agile design favors individuals and interactions over processes and tools; working, useful designs over intrusive, excessive documentation; collaboration over negotiation; and responding to change over following a plan (Sofeast. com, n.d.).

When our unit plans, curriculum maps, or daily lesson plans become too detailed or overarticulated, we face the very real danger of what Lanier (2010) calls "lock-in." This is what happens when a model, process, or protocol becomes "brittle," overrun by rules and constraints that impede one's use or revision of the program, product, or process-- or, for teachers, the unit, map, or lesson plan (p. 9). I have seen curriculum maps so intricate and impenetrable in their design that they reminded me of the Tokyo train schedules I once tried to use (in Japanese, which I did not speak or read) to get from one place to another.

Agile Yet Intentional

The tools, techniques, and templates that follow are meant to provide you a way to be agile but intentional and effective in your design process for units and daily lesson plans. Because of the innumerable realities of teachers when it comes to subject matter, grade level, class size, schedules, students, and other constraints that impinge on our design process and teaching situation, it is difficult for me to offer solutions that meet all needs, fit all contexts, or reflect all teachers' styles. On the pages that follow, you will find solutions you can adapt or adopt according to your own needs. These solutions are designed to help you, as they have done for me, think about who, what, how, and why you are teaching and, in the process, make your teaching a bit better each day as a result of becoming more intentional in what you teach and how you teach it.

> online resources | You can find all of these resources online and download them or plug them into your digital LMS: **resources.corwin.com/daybyday**.

A final thought about design-thinking and the problems we are using it to solve. In his wonderful book *The Checklist Manifesto: How to Get Things Done*, Gawande (2009) describes the three different types of problems identified by those who study the science of complexity: the simple, the complicated, and the complex. "Simple problems" are straightforward and have known solutions. For example, how to bake a cake. In other words, as Gawande concludes, "there is a recipe." "Complicated problems" can sometimes be reduced to a string of simple problems; however, because there is not a known solution, such problems tend to require more than one person, specialized knowledge and skills, and other forms of expertise. "Unanticipated difficulties," Gawande notes, "are frequent" when we encounter complicated problems (p. 49).

While it may seem like designing a unit or lesson plan that is agile, engaging, and effective for all of our students is a "complicated problem," it is not; to teach a child in a classroom filled with (in my case) thirty-four other children, is inevitably a "complex problem." Once you learn how to solve a simple or complicated problem, you can pretty much repeat the process going forward and expect a consistent solution. However, complex problems, such as teaching (or raising) a child, are, Gawande insists, fundamentally complex because each child is unique. "Although [teaching] one child may provide experience, it does not guarantee success with the next child. Expertise is valuable but most certainly not sufficient. Indeed, the next child may require an entirely different approach from the previous one, [which] brings up another feature of complex problems: their outcomes remain highly uncertain. Yet we all know that it is possible to [teach] a child well. It's complex, that's all" (p. 49).

So, as you design your units and lesson plans, keep this in mind: The work is complex, but with persistence, patience, and practice, you will improve a bit each day into the sort of expert teacher Dunn and Hattie (2022) describe in *Developing Teaching Expertise*: "Expert teachers know the limits of their knowledge and are able to seek help; they continually learn and collaborate with others in diagnosing, problem-solving, and evaluating the impact of [their] chosen solutions" (p. 115).

NOTES

Before you begin using the tools and templates provided here, I suggest that you review the Six Commitments in the Preparing to Teach section (pp. 12–15) and use them to guide your thinking as you design your units and daily lessons. In addition to revisiting the commitments, I recommend that you use the following Ten Ts of Teaching I developed to informally monitor and evaluate the demands and effectiveness of the units and assignments you create. Though these Ten Ts focus on literacy in general, they can be easily adapted to other subject areas. In short, the Ten Ts function as an informal checklist of things to consider when designing units and daily lesson plans—or reviewing why a unit or lesson went well (or wrong).

The Ten Ts of Teaching: Things to Consider When Designing Units and Daily Lessons

Text(s) what students read, view, watch, or listen to in the context of a unit or assignment; what they read and then demonstrate their understanding of

Topic(s) what students investigate, learn about, seek to understand or develop their own position about as they read a range of texts related to this topic

Time the amount of time the teacher will have or students will need to read and do the assignments related to the text(s) for this unit at the expected level

Task(s) the skills or actions students must learn or use when reading, writing, thinking, or talking about the assigned text(s) in the context of the unit

Technique(s) the strategies or approaches students use to read texts to understand, make use of, write about, or discuss those texts in the context of an assignment

Teaching the strategies and technologies (or other tools) teachers use to teach and develop skills and provide the support needed for all to succeed on an assignment

Teens what teachers need to consider and do regarding students' cognitive, cultural, and social-emotional needs when considering the other nine Ts

Thinking the types, levels, and ways of thinking required of students when reading, writing about, discussing, or being tested about the text(s) from this unit

Transfer the ability of students to ACT: **Acquire** knowledge of concepts; **Connect** those concepts in relationship to each other; **Transfer** that knowledge to new situations (see Stern et al., 2021)

Testing what teachers intend for students to learn and how they will assess the degree to which students have learned such knowledge and skills in the context of this unit and its assigned texts and tasks

Before proceeding, consider returning to the thinking you did in "Look Long: Unit Planning for this Year" (pp. 30–33) to review the initial drafts and notes you have already jotted down. I have included four Unit Design Templates here to use (a thumbnail of the template appears below); more of the templates can be downloaded from the *Teaching Better Day by Day* website.

UNIT DESIGN TEMPLATE
Essential question or understanding for the unit:

Note: Please go to the companion website for examples and detailed guidance about how to use this template.

Class _____ Unit Title/Focus _____ Projected Dates/Duration _____

1. DESCRIBE: Who Am I Teaching?	2. IDENTIFY: What Am I Teaching and Why?	3. ASSESS: Where Are They as Learners?
Think of your students as "users" of you, your class, your curriculum, your methods, materials, and assessments. Describe the five main types of students in your class and their characteristics as learners; do so without using labels or stereotypes.	Describe the standards, skills, knowledge, or habits of mind that you expect students to learn and transfer from/to other units, other classes, or the real world. Explain how they will use the skills and knowledge in this unit in and outside of school.	List the assessments and assignments that meet students where they are, clarify what they need to learn, and align with the intended outcomes specified in step 2. Make clear, with examples or rubrics, what you will accept as evidence that they learned.

User persona 1: _____

User persona 2: _____

User persona 3: _____

User persona 4: _____

User persona 5: _____

POSSIBLE ACCOMMODATIONS
Differentiate for students as needed:
☐ what or how they learn the content
☐ how they access or make sense of content
☐ how they show what they learn and can do
☐ the environment in which they learn
☐ the time needed to learn or complete a task

CULTURAL CONSIDERATIONS
☐ Do students have a voice or choice in this unit?
☐ Does this unit connect to student experiences?
☐ What difficult questions/topics might arise?
☐ Will students be allowed to collaborate?
☐ Does this unit invite multiple perspectives?

222

UNIT DESIGN TEMPLATE

4. DECIDE: How Should I Teach This?	5. ASSESS: What and How Well Did They Learn?	6. REFLECT: What to Transfer or Reteach?
Choose the experiences, instructional tools, techniques, texts, and technology best suited to teach the specific learning intentions to your students. Will all be engaged? Will all find these accessible, respectful, and equitable?	Use the assessments from step 3 to measure how well students understand and can apply what they learned about the standards from step 2. How well can they explain, interpret, apply, or take different perspectives on what they learned?	Reflect on who did and did not learn or perform as expected. Examine what and how to reteach and support those students. What should you keep in mind as you design the next unit? How can you improve this unit next time?

223

Detailed examples of sample units and lesson plans, with commentary and suggestions, using the templates below are available online at **resources.corwin.com/daybyday**.

Use the following checklist to increase the likelihood that each day's lesson may be effective. As Gawande (2009) wrote of checklists in his study of their use by doctors to solve complex problems, "you want to make sure to get the stupid stuff right, [yet] you also want to leave room for craft and judgment and the ability to respond to unexpected difficulties that arise along the way" (p. 51). So, I did my best to consolidate all that I learned into a checklist of the ten things that we could do to be a better teacher than we were the day before.

The TEN: An Instructional Checklist

- ☐ Establish and communicate clear, specific learning objectives anchored in standards.

- ☐ Integrate assessment throughout the unit and daily lesson(s).

- ☐ Teach relevant background knowledge, skills, academic language, and literacies.

- ☐ Ensure the necessary physical, emotional, and intellectual conditions for learning.

- ☐ Demystify practices and assignments by modeling, providing examples, and giving clear directions.

- ☐ Use the gradual release model of instruction: I do, we do, you do.

- ☐ Use multiple methods, modes, and media to help them learn, remember, and apply what you teach.

- ☐ Develop students' ability to generate a range of ideas, interpretations, questions, connections, responses, and solutions.

- ☐ Make explicit connections to students' lives, texts, the world, and workplace.

- ☐ Provide meaningful opportunities to practice, perfect, and perform.

You will find two versions of the Daily Lesson Template in this section. The first, The Daily Agenda, appears here in print but is a digital template of the document I use every day. In short, I write up my daily lesson plan with my students as the intended audience or users of the document, which I either project on a screen or direct them to open up on their laptops. (You can see samples and detailed explanations of the Daily Agenda on the *Teaching Better Day by Day* website.) My Daily Agenda ends up being one Google Doc with a hot-linked table of contents that takes students (or colleagues or parents—it is available to all of these stakeholders) to the Daily Agenda for that date. When students click on a specific date, the link takes them to that day's Daily Agenda, the contents of which I subsequently copy and paste (along with the link) to Canvas for that day's homework.

 Download a printable version of these templates from the companion website. You'll also find detailed examples of these templates, with commentary and suggestions, at **resources.corwin.com/daybyday**.

Here is a sample Daily Agenda so you have a sense of what this looks like in my class.

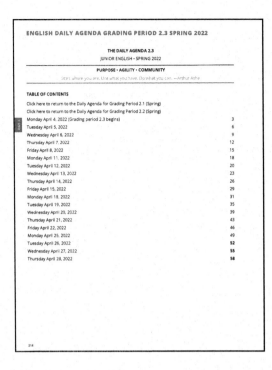

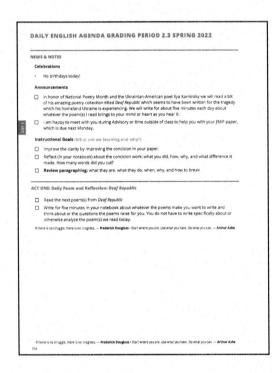

DAILY ENGLISH AGENDA GRADING PERIOD 2.3 SPRING 2022

NEWS & NOTES

Celebrations

- No birthdays today!

Announcements

☐ In honor of National Poetry Month and the Ukrainian-American poet Ilya Kaminsky we will read a bit of his amazing poetry collection titled *Deaf Republic* which seems to have been written for the tragedy which his homeland Ukraine is experiencing. We will write for about five minutes each day about whatever the poem(s) I read brings to your mind or heart as you hear it.

☐ I am happy to meet with you during Advisory or time outside of class to help you with your JRAP paper, which is due next Monday.

Instructional Goals (What are we learning and why?)

☐ Improve the clarity by improving the concision in your paper.
☐ Reflect (in your notebook) about the concision work: what you did, how, why, and what difference it made. How many words did you cut?
☐ Review paragraphing: what they are, what they do, when, why, and how to break

ACT ONE: Daily Poem and Reflection: *Deaf Republic*

☐ Read the next poem(s) from *Deaf Republic*
☐ Write for five minutes in your notebook about whatever the poems make you want to write and think about or the questions the poems raise for you. You do not have to write specifically about or otherwise analyze the poem(s) we read today.

If there is no struggle, there is no progress. — Frederick Douglass • Start where you are. Use what you have. Do what you can. — Arthur Ashe
216

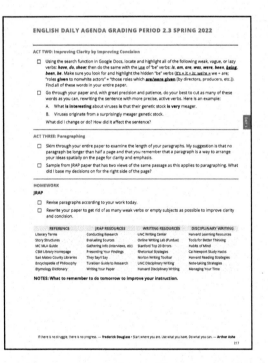

ENGLISH DAILY AGENDA GRADING PERIOD 2.3 SPRING 2022

ACT TWO: Improving Clarity by Improving Concision

☐ Using the search function in Google Docs, locate and highlight all of the following weak, vague, or lazy verbs: *have, do, show;* then do the same with the use of "be" verbs (*it's = it + is; we're = we + are;* "roles given to nonwhite actors" = "those roles which *are/were given* (by directors, producers, etc.]). Find all of these words in your entire paper.

☐ Go through your paper and, with great precision and patience, do your best to cut as many of these words as you can, rewriting the sentence with more precise, active verbs. Here is an example:
  A. What *is interesting* about viruses *is* that their genetic stock *is very* meager.
  B. Viruses originate from a surprisingly meager genetic stock.
  What did I change or do? How did it affect the sentence?

ACT THREE: Paragraphing

☐ Skim through your entire paper to examine the length of your paragraphs. My suggestion is that no paragraph be longer than half a page and that you remember that a paragraph is a way to arrange your ideas spatially on the page for clarity and emphasis.
☐ Sample from JRAP paper that has two views of the same passage as this applies to paragraphing. What did I base my decisions on for the right side of the page?

HOMEWORK
JRAP

☐ Revise paragraphs according to your work today.
☐ Rewrite your paper to get rid of as many weak verbs or empty subjects as possible to improve clarity and concision.

REFERENCE	JRAP RESOURCES	WRITING RESOURCES	DISCIPLINARY WRITING
Literary Terms	Conducting Research	UNC Writing Center	Harvard Learning Resources
Story Structures	Evaluating Sources	Online Writing Lab (Purdue)	Tools for Better Thinking
MC MLA Guide	Gathering Info (interviews, etc)	Stanford Top 20 Errors	Habits of Mind
CSM Library Homepage	Presenting Your Findings	Rhetorical Strategies	Cal Newport Study Hacks
San Mateo County Libraries	They Say/I Say	Norton Writing Toolbar	Harvard Reading Strategies
Encyclopedia of Philosophy	Turabian Guide to Research	UNC Disciplinary Writing	Note-taking Strategies
Etymology Dictionary	Writing Your Paper	Harvard Disciplinary Writing	Managing Your Time

NOTES: What to remember to do tomorrow to improve your instruction.

If there is no struggle, there is no progress. — Frederick Douglass • Start where you are. Use what you have. Do what you can. — Arthur Ashe
217

Note: These two pages form the Daily Agenda for my class on Wednesday, April 13. After each six-week grading period, I create a new Daily Agenda so the document does not get too long and cumbersome to use. The resource links at the end change over the course of the year depending on what students are doing or learning

I print out each day's Daily Agenda to use in class and put that in a binder. Along with that day's Daily Agenda, I put copies of any handouts and samples of student work from assignments I might be returning that day so that I have examples to use in the future (or show to any students who might think their work warranted a higher grade). I also include anything from that day—annotated texts I may have used, notes for teaching, bulletins or memos that seem worth keeping as part of the record of my day, even notes from students on some special occasion, or some artifact I want to remember, such as the invitation for a former student's wedding. In this way, my Daily Agenda becomes a digital record of what I did, and the binder serves as a sort of portfolio, scrapbook, and souvenir of my work. Though I do not always do it, I try to take a few minutes at the end of each day to jot down on my printed Daily Agenda any observations or insights that come to mind as I reflect back on the day.

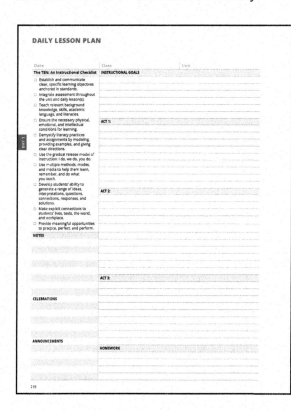

The second version of the Daily Lesson Template you find in this section is a single page you can photocopy or print directly from the online resources. It is meant to serve as an alternative when I have not been able to write up the Daily Agenda as described above or when the day's class, for whatever reason, needs only a few notes and reminders to refer to. Though this is rare, an example might be for a field trip when I need more of a working to-do list that I can keep on-hand and refer to as needed. This abbreviated Daily Agenda is still, however, designed to prompt me toward being more effective than I might otherwise be through its features and the inclusion of the instructional checklist.

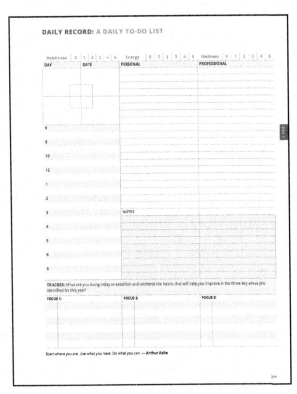

Not intended as a lesson plan template, the Daily Record is a document I designed for daily use at school. I created it to help me stay focused but also to keep an eye on myself and the demands on me. What gets scheduled is what gets done—or at least is more *likely* to get done amid the whirlwind of daily demands that accompany us through our days. The quad in the top left corner helps me focus on the four key areas of my day or four aspects of the one focus I can put at the center. See the online resources to download or print more copies or read more about how and why to use such a daily planning page.

Download a printable version of these templates from the companion website. You'll also find detailed examples of these templates, with commentary and suggestions, at **resources.corwin.com/daybyday**.

UNIT DESIGN TEMPLATE

Essential question or understanding for the unit:

Note: Please go to the companion website for examples and detailed guidance about how to use this template.

Class   Unit Title/Focus   Projected Dates/Duration

1. DESCRIBE: Who Am I Teaching?	2. IDENTIFY: What Am I Teaching and Why?	3. ASSESS: Where Are They as Learners?
Think of your students as "users" of you, your class, your curriculum, your methods, materials, and assessments. Describe the five main types of students in your class and their characteristics as learners; do so without using labels or stereotypes.	Describe the standards, skills, knowledge, or habits of mind that you expect students to learn and transfer from/to other units, other classes, or the real world. Explain how they will use the skills and knowledge in this unit in and outside of school.	List the assessments and assignments that meet students where they are, clarify what they need to learn, and align with the intended outcomes specified in step 2. Make clear, with examples or rubrics, what you will accept as evidence that they learned.
User persona 1: _____		
User persona 2: _____		
User persona 3: _____		
User persona 4: _____		
User persona 5: _____		
POSSIBLE ACCOMMODATIONS Differentiate for students as needed: ☐ what or how they learn the content ☐ how they access or make sense of content ☐ how they show what they learn and can do ☐ the environment in which they learn ☐ the time needed to learn or complete a task		
CULTURAL CONSIDERATIONS ☐ Do students have a voice or choice in this unit? ☐ Does this unit connect to student experiences? ☐ What difficult questions/topics might arise? ☐ Will students be allowed to collaborate? ☐ Does this unit invite multiple perspectives?		

UNIT DESIGN TEMPLATE

4. DECIDE: How Should I Teach This?	5. ASSESS: What and How Well Did They Learn?	6. REFLECT: What to Transfer or Reteach?
Choose the experiences, instructional tools, techniques, texts, and technology best suited to teach the specific learning intentions to your students. Will all be engaged? Will all find these accessible, respectful, and equitable?	Use the assessments from step 3 to measure how well students understand and can apply what they learned about the standards from step 2. How well can they explain, interpret, apply, or take different perspectives on what they learned?	Reflect on who did and did not learn or perform as expected. Examine what and how to reteach and support those students. What should you keep in mind as you design the next unit? How can you improve this unit next time?

DAILY

UNIT DESIGN TEMPLATE
Essential question or understanding for the unit:

Note: Please go to the companion website for examples and detailed guidance about how to use this template.

Class   Unit Title/Focus   Projected Dates/Duration

1. DESCRIBE: Who Am I Teaching?	2. IDENTIFY: What Am I Teaching and Why?	3. ASSESS: Where Are They as Learners?
Think of your students as "users" of you, your class, your curriculum, your methods, materials, and assessments. Describe the five main types of students in your class and their characteristics as learners; do so without using labels or stereotypes.	Describe the standards, skills, knowledge, or habits of mind that you expect students to learn and transfer from/to other units, other classes, or the real world. Explain how they will use the skills and knowledge in this unit in and outside of school.	List the assessments and assignments that meet students where they are, clarify what they need to learn, and align with the intended outcomes specified in step 2. Make clear, with examples or rubrics, what you will accept as evidence that they learned.
User persona 1: _____		
User persona 2: _____		
User persona 3: _____		
User persona 4: _____		
User persona 5: _____		

POSSIBLE ACCOMMODATIONS
Differentiate for students as needed:
☐ what or how they learn the content
☐ how they access or make sense of content
☐ how they show what they learn and can do
☐ the environment in which they learn
☐ the time needed to learn or complete a task

CULTURAL CONSIDERATIONS
☐ Do students have a voice or choice in this unit?
☐ Does this unit connect to student experiences?
☐ What difficult questions/topics might arise?
☐ Will students be allowed to collaborate?
☐ Does this unit invite multiple perspectives?

UNIT DESIGN TEMPLATE

4. DECIDE: How Should I Teach This?	5. ASSESS: What and How Well Did They Learn?	6. REFLECT: What to Transfer or Reteach?
Choose the experiences, instructional tools, techniques, texts, and technology best suited to teach the specific learning intentions to your students. Will all be engaged? Will all find these accessible, respectful, and equitable?	Use the assessments from step 3 to measure how well students understand and can apply what they learned about the standards from step 2. How well can they explain, interpret, apply, or take different perspectives on what they learned?	Reflect on who did and did not learn or perform as expected. Examine what and how to reteach and support those students. What should you keep in mind as you design the next unit? How can you improve this unit next time?

DAILY

UNIT DESIGN TEMPLATE
Essential question or understanding for the unit:

Note: Please go to the companion website for examples and detailed guidance about how to use this template.

Class	Unit Title/Focus	Projected Dates/Duration

1. DESCRIBE: Who Am I Teaching?	2. IDENTIFY: What Am I Teaching and Why?	3. ASSESS: Where Are They as Learners?
Think of your students as "users" of you, your class, your curriculum, your methods, materials, and assessments. Describe the five main types of students in your class and their characteristics as learners; do so without using labels or stereotypes.	Describe the standards, skills, knowledge, or habits of mind that you expect students to learn and transfer from/to other units, other classes, or the real world. Explain how they will use the skills and knowledge in this unit in and outside of school.	List the assessments and assignments that meet students where they are, clarify what they need to learn, and align with the intended outcomes specified in step 2. Make clear, with examples or rubrics, what you will accept as evidence that they learned.
User persona 1: _____		
User persona 2: _____		
User persona 3: _____		
User persona 4: _____		
User persona 5: _____		
POSSIBLE ACCOMMODATIONS Differentiate for students as needed: ☐ what or how they learn the content ☐ how they access or make sense of content ☐ how they show what they learn and can do ☐ the environment in which they learn ☐ the time needed to learn or complete a task		
CULTURAL CONSIDERATIONS ☐ Do students have a voice or choice in this unit? ☐ Does this unit connect to student experiences? ☐ What difficult questions/topics might arise? ☐ Will students be allowed to collaborate? ☐ Does this unit invite multiple perspectives?		

UNIT DESIGN TEMPLATE

4. DECIDE: How Should I Teach This?	5. ASSESS: What and How Well Did They Learn?	6. REFLECT: What to Transfer or Reteach?
Choose the experiences, instructional tools, techniques, texts, and technology best suited to teach the specific learning intentions to your students. Will all be engaged? Will all find these accessible, respectful, and equitable?	Use the assessments from step 3 to measure how well students understand and can apply what they learned about the standards from step 2. How well can they explain, interpret, apply, or take different perspectives on what they learned?	Reflect on who did and did not learn or perform as expected. Examine what and how to reteach and support those students. What should you keep in mind as you design the next unit? How can you improve this unit next time?

DAILY

UNIT DESIGN TEMPLATE

Essential question or understanding for the unit:

Note: Please go to the companion website for examples and detailed guidance about how to use this template.

Class   Unit Title/Focus   Projected Dates/Duration

DAILY

1. DESCRIBE: Who Am I Teaching?	2. IDENTIFY: What Am I Teaching and Why?	3. ASSESS: Where Are They as Learners?
Think of your students as "users" of you, your class, your curriculum, your methods, materials, and assessments. Describe the five main types of students in your class and their characteristics as learners; do so without using labels or stereotypes.	Describe the standards, skills, knowledge, or habits of mind that you expect students to learn and transfer from/to other units, other classes, or the real world. Explain how they will use the skills and knowledge in this unit in and outside of school.	List the assessments and assignments that meet students where they are, clarify what they need to learn, and align with the intended outcomes specified in step 2. Make clear, with examples or rubrics, what you will accept as evidence that they learned.
User persona 1: _____		
User persona 2: _____		
User persona 3: _____		
User persona 4: _____		
User persona 5: _____		

POSSIBLE ACCOMMODATIONS
Differentiate for students as needed:
- ☐ what or how they learn the content
- ☐ how they access or make sense of content
- ☐ how they show what they learn and can do
- ☐ the environment in which they learn
- ☐ the time needed to learn or complete a task

CULTURAL CONSIDERATIONS
- ☐ Do students have a voice or choice in this unit?
- ☐ Does this unit connect to student experiences?
- ☐ What difficult questions/topics might arise?
- ☐ Will students be allowed to collaborate?
- ☐ Does this unit invite multiple perspectives?

UNIT DESIGN TEMPLATE

4. DECIDE: How Should I Teach This?	5. ASSESS: What and How Well Did They Learn?	6. REFLECT: What to Transfer or Reteach?
Choose the experiences, instructional tools, techniques, texts, and technology best suited to teach the specific learning intentions to your students. Will all be engaged? Will all find these accessible, respectful, and equitable?	Use the assessments from step 3 to measure how well students understand and can apply what they learned about the standards from step 2. How well can they explain, interpret, apply, or take different perspectives on what they learned?	Reflect on who did and did not learn or perform as expected. Examine what and how to reteach and support those students. What should you keep in mind as you design the next unit? How can you improve this unit next time?

DAILY

DAILY AGENDA

NEWS & NOTES

Birthdays

-

-

Announcements

-

-

Instructional Notes (Why are we doing and learning this stuff today?)

-

-

-

ACT ONE: TBD

-

-

-

ACT TWO: TBD

-

-

-

ACT THREE: TBD

-

-

-

If there is no struggle, there is no progress. — **Frederick Douglass** • Start where you are. Use what you have. Do what you can. — **Arthur Ashe**

DAILY AGENDA

HOMEWORK

-
-
-
-

RESOURCES

RESOURCES	RESOURCES	RESOURCES	RESOURCES

NOTES: What to remember to do tomorrow to improve your instruction.

If there is no struggle, there is no progress. — **Frederick Douglass** • Start where you are. Use what you have. Do what you can. — **Arthur Ashe**

231

DAILY LESSON PLAN

Date	Class	Unit

The TEN: An Instructional Checklist	INSTRUCTIONAL GOALS

☐ Establish and communicate clear, specific learning objectives anchored in standards.

☐ Integrate assessment throughout the unit and daily lesson(s).

☐ Teach relevant background knowledge, skills, academic language, and literacies.

☐ Ensure the necessary physical, emotional, and intellectual conditions for learning.

ACT 1:

☐ Demystify literacy practices and assignments by modeling, providing examples, and giving clear directions.

☐ Use the gradual release model of instruction: I do, we do, you do.

☐ Use multiple methods, modes, and media to help them learn, remember, and do what you teach.

☐ Develop students' ability to generate a range of ideas, interpretations, questions, connections, responses, and solutions.

ACT 2:

☐ Make explicit connections to students' lives, texts, the world, and workplace.

☐ Provide meaningful opportunities to practice, perfect, and perform.

NOTES

ACT 3:

CELEBRATIONS

ANNOUNCEMENTS

HOMEWORK

DAILY

DAILY RECORD: A DAILY TO-DO LIST

Readiness	0	1	2	3	4	5	Energy	0	1	2	3	4	5	Wellness	0	1	2	3	4	5

DAY	DATE	PERSONAL	PROFESSIONAL
6			
8			
10			
12			
1			
2			
3		NOTES	
4			
5			
6			
8			

TRACKER: What are you doing today to establish and reinforce the habits that will help you improve in the three key areas you identified for this year?

FOCUS 1:	FOCUS 2:	FOCUS 3:

Start where you are. Use what you have. Do what you can. — **Arthur Ashe**

 Download this template and other daily pages from **resources.corwin.com/daybyday**.

REFERENCES

Abrams, J. (2009). *Having hard conversations*. Corwin.

Brown, B. (2021). *Atlas of the heart: Mapping meaningful connection and the language of human experience*. Random House.

Burke, J., & Gilmore, B. (2016). *Academic moves for college and career readiness*. Corwin.

Burkeman, O. (2021). *Four thousand weeks: Time management for mortals*. Farrar, Straus and Giroux.

California Department of Education. (n.d.). *Definition of MTSS*. https://www.cde.ca.gov/ci/cr/ri/mtsscomprti2.asp

Chardin, M., & Novak, K. (2021). *Equity by design: Delivering on the power and promise of UDL*. Corwin.

Clear, J. (2018). *Atomic habits: An easy and proven way to build good habits and break bad ones*. Avery.

Curwin, R. L., & Mendler, A. N. (1988). *Discipline with dignity: New challenges, new solutions*. Association for Supervision and Curriculum Development.

Daniels, S., & Steineke, N. (2014). *Teaching the social skills of academic interaction, Grades 4–12: Step-by-step lessons for respect, responsibility, and results*. Corwin.

Deming Institute. (n.d.). *PDSA*. Retrieved September 29, 2022, from https://deming.org/explore/pdsa

Duckworth, Angela. (2016). *Grit: The power of passion and perseverance*. Scribner.

Dunn, R., & Hattie, J. (2022). *Developing teaching expertise: A guide to adaptive professional learning design*. Corwin.

Dweck, C. (2007). *Mindset: The new psychology of success*. Ballantine Books.

Eisenhower. (n.d.). *Introducing the Eisenhower matrix*. Retrieved September 29, 2022, from https://www.eisenhower.me/eisenhower-matrix/

Feldman, J. (2019). *Grading for equity: What it is, why it matters, and how it can transform schools and classrooms*. Corwin.

Fisher, D., Flories, K., Nagel, D., Almarode, J., & Frey, N. (2019). *The PLC+ playbook, grades K–12: A hands-on guide to collectively improving student learning*. Corwin.

Fisher, D., Frey, N., Almarode, J., Flories, K., & Nagel, D. (2020). *PLC+: Better decisions and great impact by design*. Corwin.

Fisher, D., Frey, N., & Quaglia, R. J. (2018). *Engagement by design: Creating learning environments where students thrive*. Corwin.

Gawande, A. (2009). *The checklist manifesto: How to get things right*. Picador.

Gibbons, S. (2018, January 14). *Empathy mapping: The first step in design thinking*. Nielsen Norman Group. https://www.nngroup.com/articles/empathy-mapping/

Graves, D. (2001). *The energy to teach*. Heinemann.

Hammond, Z. (2014). *Culturally responsive teaching and the brain: Promoting authentic engagement and rigor among culturally and linguistically diverse students*. Corwin.

Hannigan, J., & Hannigan, H. (2021). *SEL from a distance: Tools and processes for anytime, anywhere*. Corwin.

Hattie, J. (2009). *Visible learning: A synthesis of over 800 meta-analyses relating to achievement*. Corwin.

Hattie, J., Bustamante, V., Almarode, J., Fisher, D., & Frey, N. (2021). *Great teaching by design*. Corwin.

Jensen, E., & McConchie, L. (2020). *Brain-based learning: Teaching the way students really learn*. Corwin.

Knight, J. (2016). *Better conversations: Coaching ourselves and each other to be more credible, caring, and connected*. Corwin.

Lampert, M. (2003). *Teaching problems and the problems of teaching*. Yale University Press.

Langer, E. J. (1989). *Mindfulness*. Da Capo Press.

Lanier, J. (2010). *You are not a gadget: A manifesto*. Alfred Knopf.

Lemov, D. (2015). *Teach like a champion 2.0: 62 techniques that put students on the path to college*. Jossey-Bass.

Lent, R. (2016). *Disciplinary literacy: Reading, writing, thinking, and doing... Content area by content area*. Corwin.

Marzano, R., Marzano, J. S., & Pickering, D. J. (2003). *Classroom management that works: Research-based strategies for every teacher*. Association for Supervision and Curriculum Development.

Mindtools (n.d.). *What are the HALT risk states?* Retrieved September 29, 2022, from https://www.mindtools.com/pages/article/HALT-risk-states.htm

Muhammad, G. (2020). *Cultivating genius: An equity framework for culturally and historically responsive literacy*. Scholastic Teaching Resources.

Newkirk, T. (2017). *Embarrassment and the emotional underlife of learning*. Heinemann.

Nuri-Robins, K., & Bundy, L. (2016). *Fish out of water: Mentoring, managing, and self-monitoring people who don't fit in*. Corwin.

Palmer, P. (1998). *The courage to teach: Exploring the inner landscape of a teacher's life*. Jossey-Bass.

Palmer, P. (2017). *The courage to teach: Exploring the inner landscape of a teacher's life, 20th anniversary edition*. Jossey-Bass.

Purely, W. (1999). *Creating safe schools through invitational education*. ERIC Digest.

Safir, S., & Dugan, J. (2021). *Street data: A next-generation model for equity, pedagogy, and school transformation*. Corwin.

Schmoker, M. (2018). *Focus: elevating the essentials to radically improve student learning*. Association for Supervision & Curriculum Development.

Shulman, L. (2016). *What teachers should know and be able to do*. National Board for Professional Teaching Standards.

Singer, T. W., & Staehr, D. (2020). "From watering down to challenging," *Breaking down the wall: Essential shifts for English learners' success*. Corwin.

Singleton, G. (2015). *Courageous conversations about race: A field guide for achieving equity in schools*. Corwin.

Smith, D., Fisher, D., & Frey, N. (2015). *Better than carrots or sticks: Restorative practices for positive classroom management*. Association for Supervision and Curriculum Development.

Sofeast.com. (n.d.). *What is agile design when developing new products?* Retrieved July 4, 2022 from https://www.sofeast.com/knowledgebase/what-is-agile-design-when-developing-new-products

Stegner, W. (1971). *Angle of repose*. Doubleday.

Steiner, E. D., & Woo, A. (2021). *Job-related stress threatens the teacher supply: Key findings from the 2021 state of the U.S. teacher survey*. RAND Corporation. https://www.rand.org/pubs/research_reports/RRA1108-1.html

Stern, J., Ferraro, K., Duncan, K., & Aleo, T. (2021). *Learning that transfers: Designing curriculum for a changing world*. Corwin.

Stigler, J. W., & Hiebert, J (1999). *The teaching gap: Best ideas from the world's teachers for improving education in the classroom*. Free Press.

Tatum, A. (2005). *Teaching reading to black adolescent males: Closing the achievement gap*. Stenhouse.

Tucker, C. (2012). *Blended learning in grades 4–12: Leveraging the power of technology to create student-centered classrooms*. Corwin.

Tucker, C., Wycoff T., & Green J. T. (2017). *Blended learning in action: A practical guide toward sustainable change*. Corwin.

Walsh, J. A., & Sattes, B. D. (2017). *Quality questioning: Research-based practice to engage every learner (2nd ed.)*. Corwin.

Whyte, D. (2009). *The three marriages: Reimagining work, self and relationship*. Riverhead.

Yeats, W. B. (1920, November). The second coming. *The Dial*.

A SAGE Publishing Company

CORWIN HAS ONE MISSION: to enhance education through intentional professional learning.

We build long-term relationships with our authors, educators, clients, and associations who partner with us to develop and continuously improve the best evidence-based practices that establish and support lifelong learning.